Exciting Writing, Successful Speaking

Activities to Make Language Come Alive

Martin Kimeldorf

Edited by Pamela Espeland

Free Spirit
PUBLISHING

Library of Congress Cataloging-in-Publication Data

Kimeldorf, Martin.
    Exciting writing, successful speaking : activities to make language come alive /
Martin Kimeldorf.
       p.   cm.
    Includes index.
    ISBN 0-915793-65-2
    1. English language — Composition and exercises — Study and teaching (Secondary) —
Juvenile literature. 2. Activity programs in education — Juvenile literature. [1. English language
— Composition and exercises.] I. Title.
    LB1631.K49 1994
    372.6'23 — dc20
                                                  93-30613
                                                   CIP
                                                        AC

Cover and book design by MacLean & Tuminelly
Index prepared by Eileen Quam and Theresa Wolner

10 9 8 7 6 5 4 3 2 1

Printed in the United States of America

The suggestions for ending a journal entry on pages 23–24 have been excerpted and adapted from
(w)Rites of Passage by Martin Kimeldorf. Reprinted by permission of the author.

FREE SPIRIT PUBLISHING INC.
400 First Avenue North, Suite 616
Minneapolis, MN 55401
(612) 338-2068

Contents

About This Book I

Part 1: Exciting Writing 3

Introduction..5
    List Writing, Power Writing, and 4-Step Writing........................5
    Journal Writing..5
    Advertising 6
    Poetry 6

List Writing 7
    The Leisure List..8
    Power Writing 9
    Turn a List into a Letter..10

4-Step Writing II
    4-Step Writing Warm-up..II
    4-Step Writing 12

Journal Writing..17
    What Is a Journal? 17
    Your Journal Makes You a Better Writer..............................18
    Add Details to Write Deeply 18
    The Journal Reading Coach 19
    Journal Writing Rules 20
    The Journal Word Count Chart..20
    Sample Journal Pages 21
    Add a Picture..22
    Endings 23
    101 Journal Writing Topics..24

Advertising 29

    What Makes It Work? 29

    Wanted: More Details 31

    Advertising Warm-Ups 32

    Writing Good Advertising Copy 34

    Creating a Newspaper Display Ad or Poster 38

    Creating a Radio Advertisement or Public Service Announcement 40

    Creating a Television Advertisement 44

Poetry 45

    Why Write Poetry? 46

    What Is Poetry? 47

    Poem Writing Exercise #1 52

    Poem Writing Exercise #2 53

    Poem Writing Exercise #3 54

    People Poems in 13 Lucky Lines 56

    PoemBuilder Survey 58

    Playing PoemBuilder 60

Part 2: Exciting Writing, Speaking and Reading 67

Introduction 69

    Home Assignment 69

    Public Speaking 69

    Theater Games and Script Writing 70

    Publishing a Classroom Newsletter 70

    Imaginative Literature and Story Assignments 70

Home Assignment 71

    Brainstorming Ideas and Identifying Your Style 72

    Drawing the Floor Plan 75

    Writing Your Essay 75

Public Speaking 80

    Getting Started 81

    Preparing and Giving a Speech 91

Theater Games and Script Writing 100

    Six Theater Games 101

    Script Writing: Dialogue, Stage Directions, Plot 105

    Drama Appreciation 116

Publishing a Classroom Newsletter 119

Imaginative Literature and Story Assignments 122
    Characterization 122
    Setting and Plot 133

Part 3: Exciting Reporting 141

Introduction 143
    Doing a Survey 143
    Easy Book Reports 144
    Writing a Short Report: The (Auto)Biography 144
    Writing a Longer Report 144
Doing a Survey 145
    Survey Question Warm-Ups 146
    Designing Your Survey 147
    Writing a Survey Report 157
Easy Book Reports and the Reading Journal 160
    Starting Your Reading Journal 160
    Writing a Short Book Report 161
    Giving an Oral Book Report 162
Writing a Short Report: The (Auto)Biography 163
    Report Writing Steps 164
    Life Questionnaire 165
    Organizing and Outlining 172
    Writing Your Outline 176
    Writing Your Introduction and Conclusion 177
    Expanding Your Outline into a Final Report 179
    Report Writing Quiz 183
Writing a Longer Report 184
    Report Writing Review 185
    Managing Your Time 186
    Choosing Your Topic 186
    Writing Questions and Identifying References 188
    Collecting and Organizing Information 191
    Writing Your Outline 196
    Writing Your Introduction and Conclusion 198
    Writing Your Report 200

Index 205

About the Author 208

About This Book

tudents often wonder, "Why do I have to learn this?" You might have asked this question in any number of classes. If you've ever asked it in an English or composition class, you'll find at least some of the answers in this introduction.

Exciting Writing, Successful Speaking is full of projects you complete by using your creativity, imagination, writing, and communication skills. As you practice and improve these skills, you'll feel a sense of pride and accomplishment when you finish each project. You'll discover that writing isn't as hard as you might think. You'll also discover that writing has many uses in real life.

Depending on the time you have and the goals your teacher may have set for the course, you may be working on many different kinds of projects. Some you might get to try include:

◆ entering contests and working with partners to produce a product

◆ writing and drawing in journals

◆ creating advertisements for newspapers, radio, and television

◆ writing poetry (using a *new* method, I promise!)

◆ public speaking and speech warm-up games

◆ drama games and play writing

◆ publishing class newsletters

◆ using flights of fantasy to describe characters and stories in books or on videotapes.

Which ones sound interesting to you? Each project is different. Many projects (like journal writing and newsletter writing) can be done often because you do them differently each time. Some projects take more time than others, and you may work on them a little each week, or solidly across a few days. (For instance, you might do a different advertising assignment two days a week until the advertising project is finished.) For each project, you produce an interesting and useful product for an audience, a grade, a customer, or someone else who will appreciate your work.

You might follow the projects in order, or you may skip around. All that counts is that you have fun and feel a sense of satisfaction as you enjoy and complete each project.

PART 1

● ● ● ● ● ● ● ● ● ● ● ● ● ● ● ● ● ● ● ●

Exciting Writing

Introduction

he projects in Part 1 of *Exciting Writing, Successful Speaking* show you how to enjoy writing as a sport. You begin with a few warm-up exercises using lists and a process called 4-Step Writing. You learn how to get more out of journal writing, and you discover how writing can be used in advertising for newspapers, radio, and television. You learn that writing poems can be painless and even fun.

All of these projects invite you to find new ways of using words. Each challenges your creativity and helps you to become a better writer.

List Writing, Power Writing, and 4-Step Writing

Do you sometimes have a hard time getting started writing? List writing is a simple technique that works for any type of writing assignment. If you can make a grocery list, then you can use this technique to your advantage. Power Writing makes it even more effective.

The 4-Step Writing process is guaranteed to make you a better writer. It's especially useful for compositions or other lengthy pieces. In this book, you'll learn 4-Step Writing by becoming a movie critic.

Journal Writing

This type of writing is often done weekly or daily for about five to fifteen minutes. It's a chance for you to keep track of your thoughts and feelings. You are not graded on grammar or spelling, but on your effort and thoughts. By writing a little each day, you'll build up your writing power. Journal writing will begin early in this course.

Advertising

Learning how to write a good newspaper or radio ad can be a fun way of practicing descriptive writing. You'll learn how to sell with words and pictures.

Poetry

Poetry can be fun and easy to write. You'll learn different ways of writing poems. (There's even a game that helps you to write poetry.) Poems to special friends, for birthdays, or about important feelings are fun to share with others. This kind of writing is best done after you have learned some descriptive writing techniques.

List Writing

ll writers face two main problems: getting started, and writing interesting sentences. The easiest way to get started writing is to put down your pen or pencil (or move away from your keyboard) and *think* before you write. Then put your thoughts into a list. A list is easy to make because it uses words or phrases instead of sentences. It's also easier to change and revise than a paragraph.

You can use lists to create interesting sentences. For example, you might be writing a letter to a friend about the weather. If you write, "It's raining today," that's not very descriptive. If you start by *thinking* about the rainy day and listing your thoughts, you'll be able to write a more interesting letter. Suppose your list looks like this:

> *lots of rain*
> *buckets of rain*
> *rivers in the gutter*
> *water pouring off of roofs*
> *feet are soaking wet*

Now you can use your list to write a more interesting description of the miserable, wet, rainy day. Your new description might read: "It's pouring buckets of rain today and turning our street gutters into rivers."

Writers make lists in many different ways. Lists are easy to make and useful in any kind of writing. They help you recall things from memory, and they help you to identify what you already know. You can ask people to look at your lists and add ideas to them. Think of this writing technique as making a shopping list of ideas before going to the paragraph store.

You'll begin by making a list about something you are familiar with and enjoy doing in your free time. Next, you'll learn several ways to expand simple sentences into powerful sentences. Then you'll learn how to combine list writing with 4-Step Writing to create interesting essays.

The Leisure List

Following is a list of leisure activities. Check any you have seen or done, or think you would enjoy doing. Use the spaces at the end to write down any that aren't included here but are important to you.

- ☐ 1. Camping or hiking.
- ☐ 2. Playing indoor games such as cards, chess, Monopoly, or Trivial Pursuit.
- ☐ 3. Doing puzzles or word games.
- ☐ 4. Playing indoor games such as ping-pong or video games.
- ☐ 5. Playing sports; being on teams or crews.
- ☐ 6. Exercising, self-defense, physical self-improvement.
- ☐ 7. Individual sports such as running, swimming, golf.
- ☐ 8. Gardening, farming, or fixing up trails.
- ☐ 9. Training, raising, or taking care of animals.
- ☐ 10. Enjoying the outdoors or watching nature.
- ☐ 11. Sitting and just daydreaming or meditating.
- ☐ 12. Building things, making things, or fixing things.
- ☐ 13. Making crafts such as jewelry, leather goods, pottery, or sweaters.
- ☐ 14. Collecting old or new things (examples: antiques, comics, coins, albums, posters, autographs).
- ☐ 15. Collecting personal things (examples: photos, matchbooks, trinkets).
- ☐ 16. Expressing my feelings artistically (examples: painting, writing, music, sculpture).
- ☐ 17. Enjoying or performing in skits, plays, or dance concerts.
- ☐ 18. Going to museums, parades, carnivals, or concerts.
- ☐ 19. Going to the library, reading books and magazines.
- ☐ 20. Taking classes or learning new things on my own.
- ☐ 21. Traveling or going for rides.
- ☐ 22. Participating in a religious activity.
- ☐ 23. _____
- ☐ 24. _____
- ☐ 25. _____

Now pick the activity you *most* enjoy doing (or would enjoy doing) and write it here: _____

_____

Power Writing

Hold on to your hat and get ready to Power Write!

1. Take out a blank piece of lined paper.

2. At the top, write the leisure activity you *most* enjoy doing (or would like to do) in your spare time.

3. Now write down as many things as you can about this activity. *You have 2 minutes.* Write down anything that comes to your mind, one per line. If your mind goes blank, write the word "blank" on a line.

4. When 2 minutes are up, count the number of things on your list and the total number of words you wrote (including "blank").

In Power Writing, you write under the pressure of the clock. You don't have time to stop and think. Just write, write, write! If your mind goes blank, don't worry; it will turn back on quickly. The point is to *keep writing* until it does. Keep your hand moving at all times. Don't let your mind interrupt with thoughts such as "I can't think of anything!" or "What can I write next?"

One student wrote this list about camping:

> *cold*
> *sleeping bag*
> *blank*
> *outside*
> *beautiful*
> *blank*
> *blank*
> *hot dogs*
> *campfire*
> *tired*

How many things are on your list? ____

How many words are on your list, including "blank"? ____

Good writers often ask other people for advice and ideas. Ask someone else to look at your list and suggest 2-3 things you can add. Do this with two more people.

How many new ideas did you add to your list? ___

How many new words did you add?___

Turn a List into a Letter

You don't know this, but an old friend of yours just won the state lottery. Your friend calls you up and says, "I remember you were always interested in camping. Do you still go camping?" You say "yes," and your friend replies, "Great, because I'd like to buy you a camping gift. What would you like?" You laugh and don't believe your friend, but you go along with the joke. Slowly you answer, "I've always wanted a camper van." The next week, to your surprise, a van is delivered to your house! You can't believe it! Naturally, you try to call your friend, only to learn that your friend just left on a world cruise. You decide to write your friend a thank-you letter....

1. Pretend that you've just gotten a wonderful gift from an old friend. It's something you've always wanted. It exactly matches your favorite leisure activity. (Is it a season ticket or a week of practice with a pro athlete? How about a 10-year program to study anything you want?)

    Name the gift: _____.

    Name the friend: _____.

2. Make a list of all the ways you hope to use this gift. Tell what you hope to accomplish with it or because of it. (Example: If your friend gave you a camper van, you might use it for traveling, living in, parties, private time, feeling special, or getting a new start in life.)

    Ways I hope to use the gift:

    _____

    _____

    _____

    _____

3. Now write a letter to your friend, thanking him or her for the gift. In your letter, describe some of the ways you'll be using the gift. Take ideas from your list. Your letter might go something like this:

    March 24

    Dear Theresa,

    I want to thank you for the camper van. How did you ever afford such a wonderful gift? It will change my life. I'll really enjoy it. I hope to use it for traveling as well as parties. I might even live in it someday. Who knows—with my new camper van, I can do anything!

    Sincerely yours,

    Elizabeth

4-Step Writing

n this lesson, you'll become a movie critic while you learn the 4-Step Writing method. It begins with making lists, goes on to creating sentences and paragraphs, and ends with revising and editing your writing.

4-Step Writing Warm-up

Anyone can be a movie critic simply by sharing his or her opinion. You're about to become a movie critic by writing about a movie you enjoyed seeing. Along the way, you'll learn the four different steps involved in writing an essay or composition. You'll use these steps again in future writing assignments.

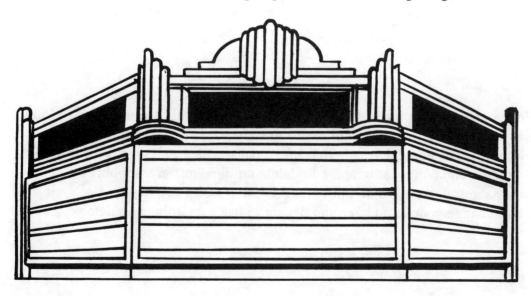

1. Think of a movie you would recommend to your friends. This can be a movie you enjoyed seeing in a theater or at home, on television or a video. Write the title on the movie marquee under the words "Now Playing."

2. If you were interviewed by a newspaper or TV reporter, what two things would you say about this movie? Keep your answers short—about 2–4 words. (Example: "It's dark and scary!") Write your answers on the movie marquee under the words "Critics Say."

3. As a critic, you have been asked to write an article recommending this movie. Follow the 4-Step Writing process described in the next section. Maybe you will want to submit your final article to the school paper.

4-Step Writing

Step 1: Prewriting
(Brainstorming and Organizing Ideas)

Start by choosing a subject for your essay—a movie you would like to review. (If you did the "4-Step Writing Warm-Up" activity, you have already done this.)

Think before you write. Power Write a list of ideas for your movie review. Write for 1 to 2 minutes, and keep your hand moving. Try to come up with at least 8 ideas. If your mind goes blank, write the word "blank."

Here's an example for the comedy *Big* starring Tom Hanks:

1. *funny*
2. *lonely*
3. *not very long*
4. *about a 13-year-old who turns into an adult*
5. *works in toy company*
6. *no friends his real age*
7. *in New York City*
8. *had to find a job*
9. *turned back into kid*
10. *I'd go again*

Next, organize your ideas. Put them in an order you think you'll want to follow when you write. You may want to group some ideas together for paragraphs, add new ideas, and delete others from your list. (As a general rule of thumb, four ideas equal one paragraph.) To delete an idea, just cross it out. Don't worry about neatness, and don't erase. Erasing slows you down. Also, you might change your mind later and decide to use something you deleted.

Here's an example for *Big*:

beginning/intro (added)

4. *about a 13-year-old who turns into an adult*

3. ~~*not very long (deleted)*~~

7. ~~*in New York City (deleted)*~~

8. *had to find a job*

5. *works in toy company*

2. *lonely*

6. *no friends his real age*

a carnival with magic (added)

9. *turned back into kid*

ending (added)

1. *funny*

10. *I'd go again*

Step 2: Writing the First (Rough) Draft

Your ideas are now ready to be turned into sentences. For the first draft, write as quickly as you can. That way, you won't get stalled. Remember, a rough draft isn't supposed to be perfect. You'll fix yours later. Meanwhile, follow these four rules. They will keep you from slowing down or stopping.

RULE #1: IGNORE SPELLING. You can go back later and correct any misspelled words. Don't slow your writing down now.

RULE #2: SKIP LINES. Write on every other line so you can add new words and ideas later.

RULE #3: KEEP WRITING. Leave blanks, lines, or question marks where you can't think of the exact word or phrase you want. Don't slow down!

RULE #4: DON'T ERASE. Make corrections by drawing a line through words or phrases, ~~like this~~. Don't stop to erase.

Here's an example for *Big*. Has the author followed the four rules of fast writing?

I wonder what it would be like to grow up in a hurry. My life would

_____?_____ You'd have to get a job. But what kind of a job? The

funny movie, the big is all about growing up fast. It could be

_____?_____. You'd have nobody to talk to your age. There was a

carnival with magic where Tom Hanks changes his age. I had lots of laughs,

especially the scene where they are eating pizza. I would go again.

Step 3: Revising the First Draft and Writing the Second Draft

Now it's time to revise your writing. You'll do this in three stages with the help of three people: yourself, a writing partner, and your teacher. During the revising, you'll get some of your best ideas, and you'll find just the right words. You'll be glad you wrote your first draft on every other line, because you'll be adding new words and ideas between the lines.

Compare the first draft of the *Big* movie review with the second draft. What specific changes did the author make to improve the writing?

FIRST DRAFT	SECOND DRAFT
I wonder what it would be like to grow up in a hurry. My life would _____?_____ You'd have to get a job. But what kind of a job? The funny movie, the big is all about growing up fast. It could be _____?_____. You'd have nobody to talk to your age. There was a carnival with magic where Tom Hanks changes his age. I had lots of laughs, especially the scene where they are eating pizza. I would go again.	*Did you ever wonder what it would be like to grow up in a hurry? <u>Your</u> life would <u>suddenly change</u>. You'd have to get a job. But what would you be <u>qualified</u> ~~able~~ to do? The funny movie "Big" is all about growing up. It could be lonely. You'd have nobody to talk to your age. ~~There was a carnival with magic where he changes his age.~~ I had lots of laughs, <u>especially the scene where they are eating pizza</u>. I would go again <u>and suggest you go too</u>.*

- ◆ In the first draft, did the author leave out any words by mistake?

- ◆ Did the author add any new words or ideas to the second draft?

- ◆ Were there any unclear sentences in the first draft? If there were, what did the author do for the second draft? (Take out the unclear sentences? Change them?)

- ◆ Did the first sentence in the first draft make you want to keep reading? (TIP: A first sentence that asks a question or tells you what the essay is about makes you want to keep reading.) What did the author do with this sentence for the second draft? (Change it? Leave it the way it was?)

Now revise your first draft. Read it out loud to yourself. This helps you to see and hear your words at the same time. As a result, you may catch more errors and get new ideas for revising. Professional writers often read their material out loud to a friend or into a tape recorder. When you hear your words, you'll get a new perspective on what you've written. It's a simple trick for improving your work.

◆ In the first draft, did you leave out any words by mistake?

◆ Did you add any new words or ideas to the second draft?

◆ Were there any unclear sentences in the first draft? If there were, what did you do? (Take them out? Change them?)

◆ Did the first sentence in your first draft make you want to keep reading? What did you do with this sentence for the second draft? (Change it? Leave it the way it was?)

Try getting some advice by reading your essay out loud to a partner.
Ask questions:

◆ Which parts were most interesting?

◆ Did I leave anything out? Was anything unclear?

◆ Would you recommend changing anything?

If your partner has good advice and ideas, include them in your essay.

Now show the teacher your revised first draft. It should be marked up with your changes and new ideas. The teacher will review the changes you have made so far and then:

◆ describe the part he or she likes best, and

◆ suggest new changes or circle things that could be changed or corrected.

Write a clean copy of your second draft, including all changes you want to make. Skip lines as you write. Show the teacher your second draft.

Step 4: Editing for the Final Draft

Now it's time to write your final draft. You'll start by editing your second draft. You want your final draft to be the best it can be, with as few mistakes as possible.

Edit your second draft with **COPS**.

Capitalization

— Capitalize the first word in each sentence.

— Capitalize all proper nouns (names of businesses, schools, brand names, geographical areas, people's names, titles of books, songs, groups, or movies, the word "I," etc.)

Overall Appearance and Style (for the final draft)

— Keep your handwriting well-spaced and legible. (If possible, use a typewriter or a word processor for your final draft.)

— Start with a clean piece of paper. Keep it neat (no smudges, tears, or extra marks).

— Use straight margins and indent the first sentence in each paragraph.

— Write a title on the top line.

Punctuation

— End each sentence with a . or ? or !

— Use commas when they are needed.

— Use complete sentences (subject and verb).

— Don't start sentences with "so," "but," "and," or "well."

Spelling

— Check words you often misspell.

— Circle any words you feel unsure about.

— Ask for help or look up the words you checked or circled.

Now write your final draft—in ink, on a typwriter, or with a word processor—and turn it in.

Journal Writing

magine that you have just finished writing a new book and it's all about *you*. Naturally, it's a bestseller. Your book could be titled *Journal* or *Diary*. Only one person has to like it—you. Be sure to write your name on the cover.

Journal writing is enjoyed by millions of people of all ages. It's fun, and it's a great way to build up your writing stamina. Soon you'll find that writing is easier than ever. If your teacher asks you to keep track of your writing on a Journal Word Count Chart, you'll see real evidence that your writing muscle is growing over time.

What Is a Journal?

We can all use a friend, and a journal can be a good friend in a busy world. Your journal is always there to listen to your innermost thoughts. It's ready when you are. Writing in your journal is like writing to your own private advice columnist.

Writing a journal entry is as easy as writing a note to yourself. The more often you write, the easier it gets. Journal writing can be fun and relaxing because it isn't graded in the usual way (if at all), and you never have to worry about spelling and punctuation. However, you may want to use your best spelling and punctuation anyway. This may be important later on, when you want to go back and read some of your earlier writings.

Many people use their journals to explore or answer questions they have been thinking about. These might be questions like:

◆ *I wonder what it will be like when I graduate from high school?*

◆ *How can I keep my attitude positive?*

◆ *What would it be like to meet a being from another planet?*

Many people use their journals to record their feelings. A journal is a great place to let off steam. You might start your writing with a sentence like:

◆ *I can't believe she would do that to me again!*

◆ *I'm so mad at myself for....*

◆ *I think I'm getting picked on when I go to....*

A journal is a place to think about how you can make important changes in your life and your attitude. In your journal, you are your own coach or counselor. Like a coach, you can try to pump up your attitude by giving yourself positive-sounding advice. You might start off by writing something like:

◆ *I hope the next time she says that to me I'll remember to....*

◆ *I'm surprised. At first I didn't think I would like....*

◆ *Today I felt more confident than ever before because....*

◆ *I surprised myself when I....*

Your Journal Makes You a Better Writer

Think of writing as a sport. Every athlete first warms up before going out and giving his or her best effort. Many writers use their journal as a warm-up activity. They know that the more often they write, the easier it gets. Some writers add to their journal every day. Others keep their journal handy all the time by leaving it near a bed, table, or desk. In the end, their journal makes them a stronger, better writer.

When you do physical warm-up exercises, it's useful to keep track of your sit-ups or push-ups by counting them. In journal writing, it can be useful to count your words. You'll quickly see that the number of words you write increases each month as you build your writing power.

Add Details to Write Deeply

The most common mistake beginning writers make is leaving out details when they write about something they are familiar with. For example, if you write about waking up in a cold room, your journal entry may not contain enough details because the experience is so familiar to you.

Today I woke up at 7:00 am. It was cold. Everyone at home and on the bus was noisy. I hope today ends well. First period was math—and we had a quiz! My mind went completely blank and I couldn't remember how to do percents.

To strengthen your writing, go beyond the familiar and the obvious. Assume that your journal is another person you are writing to. Then assume that this "other person" has no previous experience with anything in your life, and therefore, you must include as many details and examples as possible. See how the description of waking up in a cold room comes alive when you add details about the sights, sounds, and feelings you experienced.

I woke up at 7:00 am. It was so cold I could see the frost on my breath. When I turned the heater on, it filled the room with a "clang clang" sound. Sometimes it feels like I live in a noise machine.

Can you add enough details to your writing to go beyond the obvious? When you write more deeply and include more details, you soon discover that your journal writing comes alive.

Try describing how you feel about yourself as a person.

I usually start each day hoping it will end well. Sometimes I spend so much time thinking about the end of the school day, I forget to enjoy what is happening right now.

Try writing some advice to yourself.

I have got to stop getting nervous about math. I can do better when I relax. So what if I make a mistake. Even if I make the same mistake over and over, lots of times you don't learn something the first time. I wonder if I could get extra help with percents.

The Journal Reading Coach

A journal reading coach is someone who reads your journal every few days. Your coach may be your teacher or someone else with whom you choose to share your writing. Your coach will not correct your writing; his or her job is simply to read it and perhaps to respond to what you write. Sometimes your coach may be very interested in what you have written, but not quite sure what some of your ideas mean. If that happens, your coach may ask you to explain what you were trying to write about. Also, don't be surprised if your coach writes comments in your journal like "Very interesting thought" or "I wish I had written that." You may ask to see your coach's journal, if he or she is writing one.

Journal Writing Rules

1. It's *your* journal, so keep track of it. Keep it in a safe place.

2. You may not read anyone else's journal without his or her permission.

3. You can write in either pen or pencil. Don't erase anything. Simply ~~cross out~~ any words you change your mind about or don't want to use.

4. You can draw and doodle in your journal when you are done writing. Some people even clip out cartoons, pictures, or articles to paste in their journals. Remember, a journal is like a photo album of your life. If you finish before journal writing time is over, try making a drawing.

5. Write your name and today's date at the top of every journal entry.

6. You will only have a short time to write in your journal. Therefore, don't take more than one minute to think about what you will write. The key is just to start writing and let the words and ideas flow. Use the Power Writing list-making technique to get started. Take a minute or two to see how many ideas you can list before you begin writing.

The Journal Word Count Chart

Your teacher may instruct you to keep track of your writing on a Journal Word Count Chart. This is easy to do and it won't take much time.

Whenever you write in your journal, write the *date* and the *month* in the spaces at the bottom of the chart. Count the number of words you wrote. In the column above the date, put a dot opposite that number, rounded to the nearest 5. As you continue to write in your journal and use the chart, connect the dots. This becomes a graph that gives you a picture of your progress.

Here is a sample Journal Word Count Chart for four days in September. On the first day, September 14, the student wrote 15 words; on the next day, September 16, 35 words; on the next day, September 18, 25 words; on the next day, September 20, 45 words.

Journal Word Count Chart

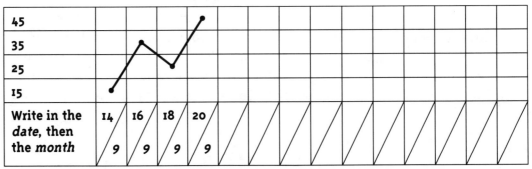

Sample Journal Pages

On September 23, this student used sentences and sometimes just words to express his feelings.

Martin Jones   September 23

<u>*BEAM ME UP I GOTTA GET OUTTA HERE*</u>

Today started out like any other day—cold and noisy in my house. It took me 30 minutes to talk myself into getting out of bed and making breakfast. My little brother was yelling at my sister and my mom yelled at me for not taking out the garbage.

    <u>*Noise*</u>

        <u>*Noise*</u>

    <u>*NOISE*</u>

And always getting hassled!!

If the rest of the day stays like this I don't think I'll last till 6th period. But I can't afford any more trouble. Otherwise I won't get the car for the game Friday night. ~~*I think this place is really*~~

I've got to get a hold of myself. What can I do.

Nothing   Nothing   Nothing????????

At least I don't have to go to the office. Jerry is always getting called down.

I think I'll visit my girlfriend. That will make me feel better. She always shares her lunch. Her dad is a great cook. But he hates me. So what—I get a great tuna sandwich out of it.

Okay, I think I can make it through the day. I've got to. Friday is almost here.

On June 3, this student started with a short doodle or picture about a question she was facing. Her picture gave her a chance to "see" her thoughts before she got started writing.

Martha Jones   June 3

<u>*The toughest question I have faced recently.*</u>

Should I move to a new school? I just can't decide. If I stay here with my relatives it may not be very fun. They are more strict. But it is hard to find new friends when you move. I know because...

Add a Picture

Your journal can come alive with drawings, doodles, and pictures. Sometimes it's helpful to start with one, like Martha did. A drawing can help you focus your thoughts when you're thinking about many things at the same time, or when you're feeling confused or unsure of yourself. Or you might end your journal entry with a drawing. Lots of writers enjoy drawing or doodling at the end of a writing session. It can be relaxing and fun. It can also help your daily word count. Some students give themselves 10 points for adding pictures to their journal entries.

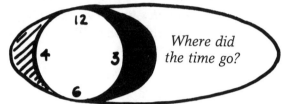

Where did the time go?

Jennifer wrote about how she uses her time. She wrote about how busy her life had become with school work, a job, and volunteer work. Here is the picture she drew when she was finished writing.

If you don't want to draw, bring in pictures you find in magazines or newspapers. Share them with the class and add them to your journal to illustrate your writing.

Mark brought in this picture. He said that sometimes he feels like an old shoe. This picture made him think of that. He brought in the picture to see if anyone else felt the same way.

If you like to draw, you can always go back and add pictures later.

How can I get out of this box???

Luther wrote about trouble he was having with his friends. He felt "boxed in" by peer pressure.

Remember: it's *your* journal. Decorate it any way you see fit. Be serious, be silly, be thoughtful, be creative. Add your own drawings or bring pictures from home. Your journal will be unique, like you.

Endings

Most journal entries describe "what's going on" in the writer's life. You can take this a step further—and get more out of your journal writing experience—by ending with a "what's next" statement. This is a good way to sum up your writing, extract the maximum amount of wisdom from your journal entry, and get good advice from an expert—you.

Start by quickly reviewing what you have just written. Then ask yourself a question or finish a statement from one of the lists that follow. Your answer will be the conclusion to your journal entry.

You may want to begin by reading through the questions and statements and checking three or more that interest you. The next time you write a journal entry, begin your ending with one of these.

To encourage reflection:

- ☐ "How did I feel as I wrote this passage?"
- ☐ "So what?"
- ☐ "What next?" ("What must I do or think about next?")
- ☐ "Why is this important to me at this time?"
- ☐ "From this I have learned..."
- ☐ "I now realize that..."
- ☐ "I really wish..."

To suggest new goals and plans of action:

- ☐ "My next step is to..."
- ☐ "I am not willing to..."
- ☐ "I guess I'm willing to..."
- ☐ "I now feel free to..."
- ☐ "I must be entering (or leaving) the stage/time of..."
- ☐ "I must now decide..."

To conclude an emotional writing session:

- ☐ "I think I am now ready to forgive myself (or another person/other people) for..."
- ☐ "I think I am not ready to give myself permission to..."
- ☐ "I need to discard an old belief in..."
- ☐ "I am really satisfied (or dissatisfied) with..."
- ☐ "What I really want out of this relationship is..."

Journal writing often focuses on something that has already happened in your life or is happening right now. You may not be able to control those events or realities. However, you *can* control your attitude toward them. You can choose how you will react to what you have written about. In choosing your attitude, you choose to be in control. Part of this involves deciding what advice you will follow. When you write in your journal, you give the advice, and you can follow it or not.

101 Journal Writing Topics

Your teacher may suggest topics for you to write about. Sometimes you will choose your own topic. You can also bring a picture, article, or idea to class that you'd like to discuss and possibly write about. Share your ideas with your teacher and decide together if they would make good journal writing topics.

Following is a list of 101 sample journal writing topics. Read through it and check any you think you might like to write about. Notice that some are left blank so you can add topics of your own.

Finish the Thought

- [ ] 1. "When I graduate...."
- [ ] 2. "I keep my attitude positive by...."
- [ ] 3. "I can't believe she/he would do that to me again! Here's what happened...."
- [ ] 4. "I'm so mad at myself for...."
- [ ] 5. "I think I'm getting picked on when I go to...."
- [ ] 6. "I hope the next time he/she says that to me, I'll remember to...."
- [ ] 7. "I'm surprised. At first I didn't think I would like...."
- [ ] 8. "Today I felt more confident than ever before because...."
- [ ] 9. "I surprised myself when I...."
- [ ] 10. "Today I feel like _____ because...."
- [ ] 11. "_____"
- [ ] 12. "_____"

Your Feelings, Life, and Interests

- [ ] 13. Do you feel like an adult yet? Why or why not?
- [ ] 14. Describe a favorite song that puts you in a special mood.
- [ ] 15. What do you enjoy doing most in your spare time?

☐ 16. What was the most important experience in your life last year?

☐ 17. How did someone help you recently? How did you help another person?

☐ 18. What is something you did well recently? What surprised you about it?

☐ 19. What is something you are good at that few people know about?

☐ 20. What is your favorite television program? Tell what characters you like best. Tell why you like them. Are they like you?

☐ 21. Do you like being alone? What do you do when you're alone?

☐ 22. What person has most influenced your life?

☐ 23. What musical instrument would you like to play?

☐ 24. What is something new you'd like to learn about this year?

☐ 25. Do you have a goal for self-improvement this year?

☐ 26. What should you do if you want to live a long time?

☐ 27. What country would you like to visit?

☐ 28. _____

☐ 29. _____

Your Friends

☐ 30. Who is your best friend? Tell what your friend likes to eat, wear, and do in his or her spare time. Tell how you are alike and different from your friend.

☐ 31. How would you describe your best friend? How would your best friend describe you?

☐ 32. What do you do with your best friend after school? What about on weekends? Do you call your friend on the telephone? Do you trade things? Do you share clothes?

☐ 33. Tell about someone you once had as a friend, but don't like anymore. What happened that caused you to break up? Do you think this could happen with other friends?

☐ 34. _____

☐ 35. _____

Your Home and Family

☐ 36. Describe the home chores you do. Which ones do you slop through, and which ones do you take pride in?

☐ 37. Who has to do the most chores in your family? Tell what each person must do.

☐ 38. How do you treat your little brother, sister, neighbor? What do you do that is nice? What do you do that is not so nice?

☐ 39. If you were in charge at home, what changes would you make that would be fair to everyone?

☐ 40. Is there someone you argue or fight with a lot at home? What was the last thing you argued about? How did you feel after the argument?

☐ 41. _____

☐ 42. _____

You and School

☐ 43. What is your favorite class? Why do you like it? How does the teacher treat you?

☐ 44. What is your least favorite class? Why don't you like it? How does the teacher treat you?

☐ 45. If you were in charge at school, what rules would you change?

☐ 46. What are your school-related goals for this year?

☐ 47. _____

☐ 48. _____

Your Community and the World

☐ 49. What is something you saw on the news recently that disturbed or upset you?

☐ 50. What is something you'd like to do to make your city, town, or neighborhood a better place?

☐ 51. What law would you change in your community?

☐ 52. If you were the mayor and your city suddenly got extra tax dollars, what would you recommend they spend the money on?

☐ 53. If you could earn school credit doing volunteer work or helping others, what would you do?

☐ 54. If you could change the world and make it a better place, what would you do first?

☐ 55. _____

☐ 56. _____

Your Gripes and Dislikes

☐ 57. What is your biggest gripe about our school? What rule would you change if you were principal for a day?

☐ 58. Have your feelings ever been hurt by someone else? What happened? What will you do the next time this happens?

☐ 59. What is the most unfair thing that happens to you? Why do you think this is unfair?

☐ 60. Describe someone you really dislike, without using his or her name.

☐ 61. _____

☐ 62. _____

Holidays and Seasons

☐ 63. What did you do over your vacation? What was the most fun? What was your greatest disappointment?

☐ 64. Describe what goes on in your house around holiday time. Brainstorm answers to these questions: What will you do to get ready for the holiday coming up? What chores will you be expected to do? Will people get crabby just before the holiday?

☐ 65. What gifts will you buy or make for others this holiday? Do you think they will like their gifts from you? How do you know?

☐ 66. What season is coming up? What will the weather be like? What do you like to do in this season?

☐ 67. Tell about the last time you went camping or got to enjoy the snow. What did you wear, what did you take, what surprise happened?

☐ 68. _____

☐ 69. _____

Sports and Games

☐ 70. What sport would you like to play or improve in?

☐ 71. What is your favorite video game to play? Tell what you like about it.

☐ 72. What is your favorite sport to watch? Why?

☐ 73. What is your favorite sports team? Who is your favorite player? Why?

☐ 74. Do you play on a school or community team? Write about your experience. Why did you decide to join the team? What do you get out of it? Do you usually make new friends when you join a team?

☐ 75. What kinds of problems do team players have? How do they get solved?

☐ 76. Do you get tired of a game after awhile?

☐ 77. What games do you like to play in your spare time? Who do you play them with? Describe how one game is played.

☐ 78. _____

☐ 79. _____

Food

☐ 80. What is your favorite place to eat? Tell what you usually order. What would you order if the sky was the limit?

☐ 81. What are some of the worst foods you have to eat? What are some of your favorite foods? Describe how you like them prepared and served.

☐ 82. Do you grow any food yourself? Tell what you do.

☐ 83. _____

☐ 84. _____

Use Your Imagination

☐ 85. If you could be in a movie, which one would you be in? What part would you play? What scene would you like to be in?

☐ 86. How would your life change if your parents won the lottery?

☐ 87. If you could change where you live, or your room, what would you change?

☐ 88. What famous person would you like to spend the day with? What would you ask him or her? What would you like to do with that person?

☐ 89. How would you like to be remembered after you die? What do you want to be known for?

☐ 90. Tell an outrageous story about why you are late for class. Make it a real whopper!

☐ 91. Imagine that your favorite fast-food chain decided to open a museum in the first restaurant they ever built. What do you think you would see there? How do you think fast food has changed in the past 20 years?

☐ 92. What would you tell a person from another planet about our society?

☐ 93. _____

☐ 94. _____

Grab Bag

☐ 95. Have you seen a cartoon that made you think? What was it about?

☐ 96. How is life easier or harder for older people?

☐ 97. What is the best way to raise and train a pet?

☐ 98. How have you helped another person recently? Who helped you recently? What happened?

☐ 99. What important problems face people your age today?

☐ 100. _____

☐ 101. _____

Advertising

riters and advertisers share the same challenge: "How can I make people believe my message?" Both must be very convincing. In this lesson, you'll learn how to create convincing advertisements. You'll practice making newspaper, radio, poster, and TV ads. You can use these skills in real life in many different ways. For example, you may want to sell something through a newspaper ad, make a flyer for a garage sale, or write an ad to pin on a supermarket bulletin board.

A good advertisement must always do three things:

1. It must get your attention.

2. It must tell you why you should buy the product or service being advertised. (How will it benefit *you*? Why is Company A's athletic shoe better for *you* than Company B's athletic shoe?)

3. It must tell you how to purchase the product or service being advertised. (What should you do next? Where should you go? Who should you call?)

Think of these as the ABCs of advertising—**A**ttention, **B**enefits, **C**all to Action— and add a D for **D**etails that will help you to accomplish all three.

What Makes It Work?

Following are ten sample want ads. Read them and circle the one that seems most interesting to you.

CHEVY CAMARO—77. Like new, kept in good condition. AM/FM radio, rebuilt engine. Call 555-1781 after 5.

JEWELRY—Daughter left town. Her party jewelry is now for sale. Cheap. If interested, mail us your address and we'll send you a price list.

POWER SAW—Sears Skilsaw. Hardly used. Makes any job easier. Only $55. Come to the garage sale May 18th.

WINTER JACKET—Wool and fur-lined coat. Nice leather outside. Recently cleaned. A steal at $45. Call Julio at 555-8976.

SPORTS EQUIPMENT—Father is leaving for Germany. Must sell all sporting equipment and supplies. You name it, I've got it. Call Jerry at 555-9080 on Sundays.

WATERBED—Like new, hardly used. Heater included. Must sell quickly. Visit the garage sale Sunday.

STEREO SYSTEM—Moving and need to sell. Large speakers, good amp. Will take any good offer. Call 555-1700.

SKATES—New wheels, new brakes. Last year's most popular design. (My feet grew.) Call 555-2425.

HONDA 1000 MOTORBIKE—New model racing bike. 4-speed with lots of gadgets. Call soon 555-8900.

ELECTRIC GUITAR—Includes amp and song books. Easy to play. I must sell quickly. Call tonight! 555-1800.

Now answer the following questions about the ad you circled.

1. How did the ad get your attention? What words made you stop and read the ad?

     _____

     _____

2. What words convinced you that this product would be worth buying? What would be the benefits to *you* of owning this particular product instead of another like it?

     _____

     _____

3. What do you need to do next to buy the product?

     _____

     _____

4. Imagine that the person who wrote the ad asked for your help to improve it. How would you make it more convincing? What details would you add? Write down at least two things you would do to make the ad work harder and better.

     _____

     _____

Wanted: More Details

Here's a very simple want ad:

> *FOR SALE BIKE*
> *Good bike for sale.*
> *Call 555-7849.*

Your job is to rewrite this ad to make it more interesting—and make the bike sound as if it's worth buying. Remember the ABCs of advertising—**A**ttention, **B**enefits, **C**all to Action—and don't forget the **D**etails.

Write a headline that will grab the reader's attention. Make it exciting! Keep it to 5 words or less.

_____

List 3-4 reasons why this bike is worth buying. Ask yourself, "What would be the benefits of owning this bike?"

1. _____
2. _____
3. _____
4. _____

Tell what the reader should do to buy the bike or find out more about it.

_____

Optional: This activity is just for fun. Do it if you have time.

Imagine that you hate to exercise in the morning, but somehow you ended up in an early-morning PE class. You want to trade for another, later class. Write an imaginary ad for your school newspaper or bulletin board. Forget about why you hate early-morning PE, and try to come up with convincing reasons why someone else might love early-morning PE.

Here's an example:

> *FOR TRADE—EARLY MORNING PE CLASS. Start your day off without having to take notes or do any reading. Begin your day by moving around. Will trade for late afternoon PE class.*

Now it's your turn:

_____

_____

Advertising Warm-Ups

Describing a Product

Many people work in advertising companies. They work in groups to come up with ads that will catch your attention. Some write the words, others do the drawing or photography, and still others write the music. Everyone contributes ideas about how the ad will look and sound.

All of the words must be powerful. They must quickly create a lasting image in the viewer's mind. These words must be like poems or song lyrics that make the reader want to do something—buy the product or service!

For this activity, your class will work in small groups of 2-4. Each member of the group brings in an advertisement from a newspaper or magazine. This should be an ad that the person thinks is especially effective—an ad that really sells the product.

1. With your group, look closely at the ads and the products they are selling. Decide as a group which product you would like to write an ad for.

2. Work together to write a new ad for the product. Be sure that your ad includes the following elements:

   On the *front* of the paper:

   a. A headline that does not include the product name.

   b. Statements describing the product's uses and benefits to the customer.

   c. Statements describing how people will feel if they buy or use the product.

   On the *back* of the paper:

   d. Draw a picture of the product. Or cut out the picture from the original advertisement and tape or paste it down.

   Don't write the product name or type anywhere on your ad.

When all of the groups are finished, the class reads the words for each ad and tries to guess the product in 4 guesses. Then they turn the page over to see the product.

Describing Yourself

Imagine that your school newspaper has a "Personals" section. The purpose of this section is to help students meet other students with similar interests, values, and characteristics. For this activity, you'll write a personal ad describing yourself. You'll want to be sure to mention your best qualities. Here's an example:

PERSONAL AD—I am looking for someone who will appreciate my talents and personality. On the outside I'm of average build, with black hair, and in good shape. Inside I am friendly. I think a lot about what I want to do and where I want to live when I graduate. I am curious and laid back. I enjoy dancing, soccer, cooking, driving, and repairing small appliances. I am always on time and very neat. In fact, my gym locker once won an award for neatness and freaked everyone out. I will not let you down because I am trustworthy. I try to help the homeless by donating cans when I go shopping. Phone me at 555-9935.

Notice that the writer uses lots of details and examples. These make your writing stronger. This same principle will help you describe your talents to potential employers, teachers, and other people you want to impress (for example, a scholarship committee).

1. Begin by interviewing a family member (or someone else who knows you very well). Ask the following questions and write down the answers.

    a. What is one of your favorite memories of me as a child?

    b. What did I do in the last two years to make you proud of me?

    c. What is something you tried to teach me to make me a better person?

    d. What is something you have learned from me?

    e. What was something I learned that surprised you?

    f. Why would someone like me when they first meet me?

    g. How am I like you?

    h. When I'm working, what is one of my best work habits?

    i. If I got married, what would I have to offer my partner?

2. Next, read the following list of words and phrases. Check any that you think describe what you are like.

☐ active	☐ energetic	☐ mature
☐ athletic	☐ friendly	☐ the outdoors type
☐ bold	☐ funny	☐ polite
☐ a book reader	☐ growing	☐ quiet
☐ careful	☐ handy with tools	☐ reliable
☐ coordinated	☐ hard-working	☐ serious
☐ creative	☐ helpful	☐ shy
☐ curious	☐ interesting	☐ social
☐ a dreamer	☐ laid back	☐ a thinker

Write five more words or phrases that describe you—the kind of person you are, things you like to do, your personality, etc.

_____

_____

_____

_____

_____

3. On a blank sheet of paper, write a personal advertisement about yourself. The purpose of your ad is to meet new people and make new friends. Describe yourself using ideas from steps 1 and 2. Add anything else that comes to mind.

   Extra Credit: Look in newspapers and magazines for pictures that could describe you. These might be pictures of people you admire, things you enjoy doing, scenery you appreciate, products you use, sports you enjoy, favorite foods or fashions, causes to which you would donate money or time, work you would like to do—anything that says Y-O-U. Create a collage with the pictures you find. Put your collage on the back of your personal ad.

4. *If you made a collage:* See how many people can recognize you first, from your collage; and second, from your personal ad.

   If you didn't make a collage: See how many people can recognize you from your personal ad.

Writing Good Advertising Copy

What makes good advertising copy? Powerful words that create lasting images in the reader's mind. Think about an advertisement you remember and like—one that created lasting images in *your* mind. This might be an ad you saw on TV, in a magazine, or in the newspaper.

Write down 3-5 things you remember about the ad.

1. _____

2. _____

3. _____

4. _____

5. _____

What made you think the product in the ad was better than other products of the same type?

_____

_____

_____

Now it's your turn.

Think of a product you'd like to sell. (TIP: This should be something you already own or would like to buy. Writing about a product you're familiar with will be easy because you probably know something about its qualities.) Then follow these steps to come up with things to say about your product. Some of the directions may not apply exactly to your product, so you'll have to be creative. Examples are given for each step.

1. Name the product you'd like to sell.

    _____

2. Tell about the benefits of buying your product.

    a. Tell how this product can save you time.

        _____

        _____

        _____

    Examples:

    "Swifty Shoes will save you time because they have quick fasteners."

    "Save time finding a special friend when you use Friendship Cologne."

    b. Tell how this product will give you enjoyment or make your life easier.

        _____

        _____

        _____

    Examples:

    "Mocha Cola will please your taste buds with its rich, chocolatey taste."

    "Wrinkle-Free Shirts never need ironing."

    c. Tell something about the quality of your product. Will it last a long time? Is it made well? What is it made of? Does it come with a guarantee?

        _____

        _____

        _____

Examples:

"Swifty Shoes will last for a full year, or until you run your tenth marathon—whichever comes first."

"I guarantee that you will like your Super Sound Stereo or your money back."

d.   Describe what your product looks like. What makes it really stand out?

_____

_____

_____

Examples:

"Swifty Shoes come in different shades of gold and silver."

"No one will miss your Super Sound Stereo because it's candy-apple red."

e.   Tell why your friends will like this product. When they see it, will they want one, too?

_____

_____

_____

Examples:

"Your friends will want to borrow your Friendship Cologne."

"Everyone will want a Wrinkle-Free Shirt just like yours."

f.   Tell why your product is easy to use. How long does it take to learn how to use it, set it up, or get it started working?

_____

_____

_____

Examples:

"You can set up your Super Sound Stereo in less than 30 minutes."

"You don't need a college degree to use the 21-speed Zoomer Mountain Bike."

g.   Tell why the price is a good deal. If your product costs more than other products of the same type, is it worth it? Prove it. Tell why.

_____

_____

_____

Examples:

"It's the lowest price in town."

"We may cost a little more, but we give you a larger tool chest."

h. Tell about any other important benefits of your product.

_____

_____

_____

3. Using the ideas you have written down, create a 6-10 line advertisement to sell your product. Write directly to your audience—use the word "you."

a. Start by writing a first (rough) draft. Remember the rules you learned in 4-Step Writing: ignore spelling, skip lines, keep writing, and don't erase.

— First, write an attention-getting headline.

— Second, list 3-4 reasons why your product is worth buying.

— Third, tell what the reader should do to buy your product or find out more about it.

Example:

KANGAROO BACKPACKS ARE A JUMP AHEAD

A Kangaroo Backpack has more pockets than a herd of mother kangaroos. There's room for your books, notebooks, calendar, pens, pencils, calculator, lunch money, keys—even a secret pocket for notes you don't want your friends to find. It's so durable it will never wear out. Plus the straps are adjustable so you stay comfortable. Hop over to the nearest More Mart store and buy yourself a Kangaroo Backpack!

b. Fix and correct your rough draft, then do a final draft in ink. Draw a picture of your product, or find a picture in a newspaper or magazine ad. Read your ad out loud to the class.

Creating a Newspaper Display Ad or Poster

Study the advertisement below. Notice that it has 5 parts. You're about to create an advertisement with these 5 parts.

NEW HEARING LOCK FOR SCHOOL LOCKERS

With this new lock, you don't need a key!

Special
Decoder
Receiver

◆ Special decoder receiver recog-nizes your voice.

◆ It unlocks and locks based on your voice command.

◆ 2 Year Warranty

◆ Only $65.00 while supplies last

1. Headline draws your attention.

2. Picture draws your attention.

3. Copy describes the product's advantages and uses.

4. Price is stated.

5. Copy tells the customer what to do next.

Visit Electro Hardware Today. Near the gas station at 5th and Plum.

What would you like to create a newspaper display ad or poster for? Here are some ideas. Check any that interest you. Then write down the product, person, or place you will create an ad for.

☐ A place you like to shop

☐ A product you use

☐ A service or business you'd like to start

☐ Something you'd like to invent

☐ A sport you like or team you want to try out for

☐ An employer you work for

☐ A class you enjoy, or a teacher or aide you like

☐   Yourself

Name your product, person, or place: _____

_____

1.   Write a headline—no more than 3-6 powerful words.

   _____

   _____

2.   Write the copy—no more than 5 lines. These don't have to be complete
     sentences.

   _____

   _____

   _____

   _____

   _____

3.   Write the price of your product: _____

4.   Tell what you want the customer to do next—phone in? Send you some-
     thing in the mail? Visit your store? What else? Describe, giving details:

   _____

   _____

   _____

   _____

5.   Describe the picture you might use for your newspaper display ad or
     poster. Your picture can be from a computer, a magazine—or you can draw
     it yourself.

   _____

   _____

   _____

   _____

6.   Create your advertisement on a clean sheet of paper.

If you're pleased with how your ad or poster turned out, consider taking it or
sending it to the company that makes the product. They'll appreciate the fact
that you thought of them.

Creating a Radio Advertisement or Public Service Announcement

Could you sell your product or get someone involved in your cause without using any printed words or pictures? That's what radio advertising does. In this activity, you'll write and produce a radio ad or public service announcement. You'll even record it to get a feeling for what it would sound like on the radio.

First, you'll need to create a *script*. A script spells out what happens in your ad from beginning to end. It includes all the words plus descriptions of the sounds and/or music you will use. If you work with a partner, you may decide to put one person in charge of the words and the other in charge of the sounds and/or music—but you'll have to cooperate to make sure it all goes together.

On pages 41–43 are two sample radio scripts, written in two different styles. Read them both, then decide which style you want to use.

◆ In the "Bill's Burger Hut" script, the words and sound effects are all written in one column, but the sound effects are written in boxes.

"Bill's Burger Hut" is a basic radio advertisement. Its purpose is to sell a product—Bill's Burgers. If reading it now makes you hungry for a burger, imagine how you would feel if you heard it right after school, at the end of a busy and exhausting day.

◆ In the "Animal Wildlife Refuge" script, the words are in the left-hand column and the sounds are in the right-hand column.

You'll notice that "Animal Wildlife Refuge" is different from "Bill's Burger Hut." It doesn't try to sell you anything. Instead, it tries to get you personally involved in a cause.

Radio advertising is a powerful tool for persuading people. Groups and individuals who believe in a cause often try to get their message out over the radio. They may not have money to buy radio time, so they create a special type of radio ad called a Public Service Announcement (PSA). Most radio stations offer free air time for PSA's.

The "Animal Wildlife Refuge" PSA was created by students who wanted to draw their community's attention to a local animal wildlife rescue and refuge center. The center cared for wild animals that had been injured or abandoned, setting them free when they were ready to return to the wild. One day a fire swept through the center. The fire destroyed animal holding and feeding areas, supplies, and part of the office. The staff was demoralized until a story about the center appeared in a local newspaper and donations started trickling in. A group of students decided to help with the fund raising effort. They scheduled a benefit car wash and created a PSA to air on a local radio station. The students raised over $500 for the center.

As you read each script, notice that the name of the place being advertised is mentioned *at least twice*.

"BILL'S BURGER HUT" RADIO SCRIPT

Announcer:

Where can you go after school for a quick bite?

Go to Bill's Burger Hut to fill up on high-energy food.

Sounds of students in the hall—then fade out.

Student #1:

I feel run down, drained at the end of the school day.

Student #2:

Me, too. I have PE last period and I've sweated out all my energy. Where can we go to refuel?

Student #1:

I go to Bill's Burger Hut!

You can fill up on a huge, juicy burger with cheese and bacon for only $2.50.

Chorus of voices hums the "Bill's Burger Hut" jingle.

Student #2:

Sounds good to me. Hey, isn't that Ellen and Marcy?

Sounds of cars quickly leaving the parking lot.

Student #1:

Yeah, and guess where they're going? We could have hitched a ride!

Sound of popular song.

Announcer:

Don't get left behind with the hungries. Go to Bill's Burger Hut for a delicious stop after school.

Music fades and chorus of voices sings the words, "Bill's Burger Hut."

"ANIMAL WILDLIFE REFUGE" PSA SCRIPT

Script	Sound cues
Announcer:	Intro sound—A rifle being loaded, cocked, and shot
One day a hunter mistakenly shot a mother Barn Owl. The hunter took the scared baby owl to the Red Fern Animal Wildlife Refuge. The volunteers took in the baby owl and gave it food and shelter.	Sound of owl
Volunteer 1:	
That's the sound of Francis, the Barn Owl. I got really involved in helping this orphan owl. Here, little fella, I've got dinner for you….	
Announcer:	Theme song for refuge—upbeat music
Soon Francis will be strong enough to be released from the refuge. But Francis will leave behind many animal friends—like Sue, the abandoned fawn; Jonah, the injured elk; and Phillip, the malnourished squirrel.	
Volunteer 1:	
I feel like I really make a difference when I come to the Red Fern Animal Wildlife Refuge.	
Volunteer 2:	
These animals don't make any demands on anyone. I feel that we owe them some help, since so many have lost their homes to local housing developments.	
Announcer:	Sounds of crackling fire, voices yelling for water, fire extinguishers, transferring animals, etc.
Volunteers of all ages put in 1 to 20 hours a week. But now they need your help.	
Announcer:	Sad music softly in the background.
Last week a fire broke out and destroyed many of the holding pens, feeding areas, and the animal hospital supply depot. The students at Timberland School want to help out, just like you do. We're holding a car wash at our school on Saturday, October 5th.	
Volunteer 1:	
I'll be there with sponge, rags, and polish. Won't you please bring in your car?	
Volunteer 2:	Sound of owl
Animals like Francis really depend on the Red Fern Animal Wildlife Refuge.	

Announcer:

The Timberland students urge you to bring your car down to our school so we can wash and polish it to your satisfaction.

Volunteer 1:

All money collected will be donated to the refuge.

Volunteer 2:

That's Saturday, October 5th, from 8 a.m. to 8 p.m. at the Timberland School student parking lot.

Theme song slowly fades in, growing louder gradually, but not overriding the words

Now it's your turn. Write your own radio ad or PSA. Follow these steps.

1. Decide on a product or cause you want to promote.

2. Make a list of things you want to say about your product or cause. Also make a list of the sounds (sound effects, music) you think might be fun to use in your ad.

3. Write a complete script. Show the words and the sounds. Leave plenty of room to change the script once you see it and hear what it sounds like.

4. Rehearse your script. Make sounds with your voice or tape record real sounds. Use prerecorded music.

5. Practice recording your script. Then tape it again for a final product.

Creating a Television Advertisement

In a television ad, the words, sounds, and/or music are combined in the Audio Script. The Visual Script describes what the audience will see. The two scripts run side-by-side. Each part, or "scene," is numbered. Directions are shown in parentheses.

Following is a sample script for an aftershave. Read it carefully, then work in a team to create your own TV ad.

"R & B SNACK CRACKERS" TELEVISION SCRIPT

Audio Script	Visual Script
1. (Music from a popular Rhythm & Blues [R & B] album comes up slowly.)	1. Closeup of product package.
2. When you want a snack, it should fit your mood.	2. Gerald pulling a sweatshirt over his head.
3. Not this way... (Loud heavy metal music.)	3. Gerald discovers that the picture on his sweatshirt is a heavy metal band, "The Screaming Psycho Fiends"—he looks upset.
4. Not this way... (Soft easy listening music.)	4. Gerald sees that the picture on his sweatshirt is a cute teddy bear—he looks even more upset.
5. But this way. (Fade in R & B music again.)	5. Gerald sees that the picture on his sweatshirt is a guitar. He looks relieved and reaches for a box of R & B Crackers.
6. With R & B crackers, you'll always feel the rhythm and you'll never get the blues.	6. Gerald eats a cracker, smiles.
7. (Music up loud, then fades out.)	7. Fade to shot of product package.

Poetry

oets work a lot with the skills you have already learned in Part 1 of *Exciting Writing, Successful Speaking:* making lists, adding details, and revising. Like advertising writers, poets must be persuasive. But instead of trying to get their readers to buy something, poets usually want their readers to *share* something: the feeling, experience, or insight that inspired them to write the poem.

Because poems are made up of phrases and words, you'll find them easy to write. You don't have to worry about complete sentences or paragraphs. You can play with words, make up new words, and capitalize (or not) whatever you want. You can use punctuation in new and creative ways without worrying about the rules.

You can turn poetry writing into a game with something called PoemBuilder. Even if you have never written a poem before—even if you're positive you *can't* write poetry—PoemBuilder makes it possible. That's because it gives you the words you need. All you have to do is answer a few questions, roll a die, and "build" your poem using word lists your teacher will give you.

Here is an example of a poem written with PoemBuilder:

MY 10-SPEED BIKE

Grand, bright 10 speed!
    Bike races and travels....
Recent Peugeot,
    sonic green
    —unnatural 2-wheeler
       riding it makes me feel enchanted.

What makes a poem or song stand out? What makes it memorable? Most people would say it's because the writer used words in new and different ways. That's what PoemBuilder helps you to do. Soon you'll be writing *real* poems you can be proud of—and having fun besides.

Why Write Poetry?

People write poems for many different reasons. Here are four possibilities. Check the one (or ones) that best describe why you think *other people* write poetry:

- ☐ To tell a story.

- ☐ To send a special message to someone the poet likes or loves.

- ☐ To sum up the poet's feelings or thoughts.

- ☐ To create a picture in the reader's mind.

What is one reason why *you* might write a poem? This might be the same as one of the reasons you just read, or it might be something new:

Read the following poems and see if you can guess the reasons why people wrote them. Write the number of the poem in front of the reason you choose.

Poem	Reason
1. *Have I ever told you* *how much you mean to me?* *The gentle way you touch my hand* *The kind way you listen* *Sets my heart free!*	___ To sum up the poet's feelings or thoughts.
2. *I'm doing time* *for committing a crime* *with a slip of the knife* *I changed my life*	___ To send a special message to someone the poet likes or loves.
3. *The rumbling machine roared down the street,* *eyeballs turned—it was quite a treat!* *The red chariot Ford shifted into auto-flow,* *smells of rubber and exhaust filled my nose.*	___ To tell a story.
4. *The sun set silently upon the hills* *flowers turned their faces to the horizon.* *As the funeral began the sun sank into the hills* *darkness swallowed us up like specks of dirt.*	___ To create a picture in the reader's mind.

Did you notice that some of the poems could fit more than one reason? When you write a poem, you never know how the reader will react. That's part of the mystery—and the power—of poetry.

Did you notice that the lines in the poems don't run on like paragraphs? The poet chooses when and where to end each line.

What Is Poetry?

Just about anything can be a poem. A poem may remind you of something from your own life. Like a favorite song, it may stir up feelings or memories. (In fact, many songs are really poems set to music.) A poem can be peaceful or exciting, happy or sad, simple or complicated, short or long. A poem can be persuasive. A poem can be whatever the poet decides to make it.

Basically, poetry is the effective use of language. A poet is never satisfied with describing pond animals as "the frogs." Instead, the poet might write about "the croaking, roaring frogs." The frogs come alive with the sounds of the words the poet chooses.

Poetry Is Sounds

Be a poet. Draw lines between the subjects and the sounds you think go with them.

Subjects	*Sounds*
cat	crinkly and crisp
music	jingles and jangles
dollar bill being folded	roaring heat
coins in your pocket	hissing s-s-s-s
campfire	heavy beat

Be a poet. Write your own subjects and the sounds you could put with them.

Subjects	*Sounds*
_____	_____
_____	_____
_____	_____
_____	_____

Poetry Is Rhythm

Some poetry has a strong beat or rhythm to it. This type of poetry is often found in songs. Think back to the first song-poem you learned as a child. It might have sounded like this:

> *Row, row, row your boat*
> *Gently down the stream*
> *Merrily, merrily, merrily, merrily*
> *Life is but a dream.*

Write a few lines from a song you like. The song should have a good beat. Write it so that each line has one or two strong "beats" in it.

_____

_____

_____

_____

Poetry Is Colors

Think of all the ways one color can be used. Match the colors to the descriptions.

Colors	*Descriptions*
___ red	1. a pie crust, sweet cider, a Gypsy's earring
___ gold	2. a cat's eyes, a tossed salad, a jade stone
___ green	3. fire engines, danger, a sparkling ruby

Write your three favorite colors. Then write three things each color could be used to describe.

Colors	*Descriptions*
_____	1._____
_____	2._____
_____	3._____
_____	1._____
_____	2._____
_____	3._____
_____	1._____
_____	2._____
_____	3._____

Poetry Is Painting with Words

Long ago, humans lived in caves and didn't have language. They wrote down their thoughts using pictures instead of words. This made it easy to create an image in someone else's mind—the pictures were there on the wall for all to see. Creating images with words can be more of a challenge.

Suppose that you could leave a message on a cave wall. You may choose three pictures from the ones shown below. Circle your choices, then write what they mean to you. Cover up your message and see if a partner can guess it from looking at the pictures you circled.

My picture message means: _____

Now read the three lines that follow. Write about the image that first pops into your mind after you read each line.

1. *My cherry-red Camaro-machine....*

The first image that pops into my mind is: _____

2. *Muscular and graceful god-like body....*

The first image that pops into my mind is: _____

3. *A field of perfumed flowers, buzzing like bees....*

The first image that pops into my mind is: _____

Poetry Is Rhyme (Sometimes)

Probably the first poetry you ever read or learned was poetry that rhymed. Words that sound alike have a special effect on the reader or listener. Below is a poem that uses rhymes:

> *People do things in different ways*
> *That's why there is color...*
> *Not just black, white, and grays.*

What is this poem about? _____

Do the rhymes make the poem easier to remember? _____

Write down two lines that use rhyming words.

_____

_____

How do poets and songwriters come up with words that rhyme? Some of them use rhyming dictionaries. Others do exercises and activities like this one:

1. Pair up with a writing partner. You should each have a piece of scratch paper and something to write with.

2. Write down two words that rhyme. Don't take any longer than 1 minute.

3. Trade papers. Read your partner's words. Add your words to your partner's paper while your partner adds two more rhyming words to your paper.

4. Trade papers again. (Each of you should now have your own paper.) Write down two more rhyming words.

5. Trade papers again. Continue for 5-10 minutes and see how many words you can write.

6. Look at your list—which now contains your rhyming words *and* your partner's rhyming words—and choose two words to use in a poem. Write them at the ends of two lines, like this:

    _____ care.

    _____ fair.

7. Complete the lines. Example:

    I know that you really care
    When you treat me fair.

Poetry Is Word Play

Poets play with words all the time; that's half the fun of poetry. Poets don't always care about grammar, spelling, or capitalization as much as they do about the meaning, feeling, or "look" of their poem. As a result, many poets invent new words. Made-up words help to make a poem special and unique.

One way to make up a new word is by connecting two words with a hyphen. For example:

The taste-exploding pizza....

Think of two words you could connect with a hyphen. You might use the name of someone famous and add a word describing something the person does. For example:

Montana-passer....(describes a famous quarterback)

Your word: _____-_____

Another way to make up a new word is by adding "-ing" to the end of a word. This turns a noun into a word that sounds like a verb. It adds action and "spin." Read these two poems, then underline the made-up "-ing" words:

> *No time to eat or play*
> *The time is booking by at school*
> *And I scan pages with radaring eyes....*
>
> *The volcano erupted*
> *and started*
> *Ash-traying the sky....*

Add "-ing" to the words below. Then write lines using your made-up words:

jelly

_____

book

_____

word

_____

pill

_____

cup

_____

Some poets capitalize words in unusual ways to draw your eye to them. One poet used this technique to write a poem for a friend named Al. Read the poem, then circle the examples of unusual capitalization.

> *Dear friend AL*
> *You have helped me so often*
> *You're a capitAL friend.*
>
> *We shared some good times.*
> *We have tALked away the hours*
> *and laughed our heads into the sky.*
>
> *I'll miss you.*
> *Why must you go college-ing?*
> *ALl my thoughts are with you.*

What is this poem about?

_____

_____

Does the unusual capitalization make the poem stand out? _____

Why did the poet choose to capitalize those two letters?

_____

_____

Poem Writing Exercise #1

Poems paint strong pictures in your mind. Read this poem about waking up and smelling breakfast being prepared. Notice that it doesn't rhyme. (Poems *can* rhyme, but they don't *have to* rhyme.)

> *The dawn broke early*
> *The alarm clock crashed through my sleepy dreams*
> *And the smell of bacon and eggs coaxed me out of bed.*

What picture does this poem paint in your mind? What does this poem remind you of? How do you feel after you read it? Write your answer to any one of these questions:

_____

_____

_____

Now imagine that it's the morning of a day when you get to sleep in. You don't have to go to school. You don't have to wake up to your alarm clock. But you wake up anyway....to feelings, smells, sights, and sounds. Answer the following questions. Try to paint pictures with your words.

How do you feel? _____

What do you smell? _____

What do you see? _____

What do you hear? _____

Congratulations—you have just written the first draft of a poem! Now it's time to revise it and polish it.

Here's an example of how this is done. Can you find all of the changes the writer made between the original poem and the revised, polished poem?

Original Poem

It was six o'clock in the morning and I didn't want to get up
because I was in a beautiful dream.
The sound of the alarm was like thunder.
The smell of breakfast got my nose out of bed.

Revised and Polished Poem

Six o'clock in the morning
I was in a beautiful dream.
The alarm sounded like thunder.
My nose got out of bed first
following downstairs to breakfast.

For the revised and polished poem, the poet cut out all the "extra" words and kept only the most important ones. Notice that some lines aren't even sentences. But each line contains *one* important idea, just like a sentence.

As you revise and polish your poem, think of each line ending with a drum beat. This will help you to put important words at the ends of lines. You won't want the drum beats to happen at random.

As you revise and polish your poem, ask yourself these questions:

◆   How will I break up my lines?

◆   Which words are the most important?

◆   Which words can I take out to make my poem stronger?

Poem Writing Exercise #2

The Japanese developed a method for writing short, 3-line poems that leave powerful images in the mind of the reader. Poems written in this way are called *haiku*. You can easily and quickly write haiku-like poems by following a few simple rules. Study the examples, then write your own.

Example A

On the first line, write the *subject* of your poem using 1-3 words.

On the second line, write about the subject's *location* using 3-5 words.

On the third line, write about the subject's *action* using 1-3 words.

> *The tree*
> *on a lonely mountain*
> *stands.*

Example B

On the first line, write the *subject* of your poem using 1-3 words.

On the second line, write about the subject's *location* using 3-5 words.

On the third line, write about the subject's *action* using 1-3 words.

> *Loren*
>
> *sitting under the apple tree*
>
> *looks beautiful.*

Example C

On the first line, write the *subject* of your poem using 1-3 words.

On the second line, write about the subject's *location* using 3-5 words.

On the third line, write about the subject's *action* using 1-3 words.

> *Basketball*
>
> *on the rim*
>
> *hesitates, then earns two points*

Now it's your turn. Write about an animal or nature.

_____

_____

_____

Now write about an object or a person.

_____

_____

_____

Poem Writing Exercise #3

Think of someone who is special to you. You're about to write a poem to that person.

The person's name is: _____

1. Start by completing the following lists. Choose words as special as the person you'll be writing about.

How the person looks/Colors that remind me of him or her

_____

_____

_____

How the person sounds/feels

_____

_____

_____

Things the person does/words he or she uses a lot

_____

_____

_____

Images or feelings I have about the person

_____

_____

_____

Things I remember about the person

_____

_____

_____

2. What rhyming words can you think of that have to do with him or her?

_____ and _____

_____ and _____

3. Write the first draft of your poem. It should be 4-8 lines long.

_____

_____

_____

_____

_____

_____

_____

4. Revise and polish your poem. Follow these steps:

    a. Decide on the best place to end each line. Put a slash mark (/) in every place where you want a line to end.

    b. Go back and play with some of your words.

        — Capitalize or underline for emphasis.

        — Make up new words using hyphens.

        — Make up new words using "-ing."

5. Write your revised and polished poem here:

_____

_____

_____

_____

_____

_____

_____

_____

People Poems in 13 Lucky Lines

Can you describe someone in 13 lines of poetry? You can when you follow these simple steps.

You'll be writing poems to two people. The first is a famous person you admire, or a famous character from a story, movie, TV show, or song. The other is a person you know in real life. For each poem, you'll use a series of "poetry line starters" provided on a handout your teacher will give you.

The famous person/character you'll be writing about is:

_____

The real-life person you'll be writing about is:

_____

I. First Draft

Complete the 13 "poetry line starters" for each person you're writing about. Pretend you *are* that person. Use your imagination. Be creative, get wild! Keep your lines short.

First Stanza

1. I am.... (Example: "I am tall and round and wear many years on my face.")

2. I hear.... (Examples: "I hear songs in my head and heart." "I hear voices that tell me what to say and write.")

3. I see.... (Examples: "I see well-dressed people standing in line to meet me." "I see rows and rows of chocolate bars standing at attention.")

4. I am.... (Repeat line 1.)

Second Stanza

5. I pretend.... (Example: "I pretend that I'm flying through the mountains.")

6. I worry.... (Example: "I worry about the future and if I'll be in it.")

7. I cry.... (Example: "I cry when I hear a sad song.")

8. I am.... (Repeat line 1.)

Third Stanza

9. I say.... (Example: "I say that I am proud to be different.")

10. I dream.... (Example: "I dream about competing in the Olympics someday.")

11. I try to make a difference by.... (Example: "I try to make a difference by helping other people.")

12. I hope.... (Example: "I hope that I can someday leave the planet and travel through space.")

13. I am.... (Repeat line 1.)

Write or type your first draft on a clean sheet of paper. Remember to skip lines.

II. Second Draft

Share your poem with another person. Discuss changes to make or new ideas to include. Decide what you are going to cut out and what you are going to add. Decide how you will change words around, make up words, or emphasize certain words. Show your revisions to your teacher.

III. Final Draft

Write or type your final (revised and polished) poem on a clean sheet of paper.

PoemBuilder Survey

You're about to play PoemBuilder, a game that makes poetry writing fun and easy. PoemBuilder actually gives you the words you need to create terrific poems. You still have to do *some* work—you have to decide which words you like and which words you don't like, what order your words should go in, whether you want them to rhyme, and so on—but everything you need is at your fingertips. You'll see your poem take shape in front of your eyes.

Start by completing this survey.

Step 1: Choose Your Topic

Think about someone or something—person, place, animal, scene, etc.—you would like to describe in a poem. (Your poem cannot be about an idea.) This should be someone or something you feel strongly about.

My poem will be about: _____

Step 2: Describe Your Topic

Is your topic big or small? Hot or cold? Loud or quiet? The words are small, but their meanings may be deeper. For example, suppose you were writing a poem about your mother. "Big" could also mean "important." "Hot" might mean "hot-tempered." If you were writing about a car, "hot" could describe your feelings about it—the "hot machine." "Loud" could describe clothing, colors, or moods as well as sounds. Someone's jacket might be a "loud yellow." A car might be "screaming fire-engine red." A flower might bloom in a "quiet pile of dirt."

Read the following groups of word pairs. For each pair, check the one word that comes closest to describing your topic. It may not "fit" exactly, but don't worry about that now. What's important is to choose one word from each pair. If you skip a pair, PoemBuilder won't work as well.

S: Senses Words

Which word in each pair best describes your topic in terms of your senses?

☐ BIG	or	☐ SMALL	
☐ HOT	or	☐ COLD	
☐ NICE TO TOUCH	or	☐ NOT NICE TO TOUCH	
☐ SMELLS GOOD	or	☐ SMELLS STRONG OR BAD	
☐ TASTES GOOD	or	☐ TASTES STRONG OR BAD	
☐ LOUD	or	☐ QUIET	
☐ SOUNDS PRETTY	or	☐ SOUNDS AWFUL	

E: Emotions Words

Which word in each pair best describes the "feeling" of your topic, or the way you feel about it?

- ☐ NATURAL (it grows)   or   ☐ ARTIFICIAL (human-made)
- ☐ HAPPY   or   ☐ SAD
- ☐ SERIOUS   or   ☐ FUNNY
- ☐ OLD   or   ☐ NEW
- ☐ COLORFUL   or   ☐ ONE COLOR
                            (write the color: _____)

N: Naming Words

Follow the directions to come up with six different names for your topic.

1. Write the official name of your topic (if a person: the full first or last name).

    _____

2. Write a nickname, slang name, or pet name for your topic:

    _____

3. Write two or three groups your topic belongs to. Examples: Apple belongs to TREES...FRUITS...FOOD. Your friend Marty belongs to MEN... STUDENTS...PEOPLE.

    _____   _____

4. Write the possessive form of your topic's name, then add a word after it. Examples: Apple's Color, Marty's Books.

    _____'s _____

5. Think of one more name for your topic. Use one of the ideas already given in the directions, or use your own idea. Can you think of a new nickname or slang word? What about another group? Is there an original naming word that describes why your topic has special meaning for you? For example, what makes your topic unforgettable?

    _____

A: Action Words

Follow the directions to come up with six different things your topic can do.

1. Write something your topic can do by itself. This must be a verb or a verb phrase. Examples: Apples RIPEN or TASTE GOOD. Mary Jo TEACHES or JOGS or LAUGHS.

    _____

2. Add "-ing" to your topic's official name. Example: Apple becomes APPLING.

_____

3. Write something you do *with* your topic. Examples: BAKE Apples. RUN with Mary Jo.

_____

4. Write three more words or phrases that describe what your topic does. Use the ideas already given or come up with your own. Examples: Car BURNS RUBBER. Marty SHARES TIME. Cat HUNTS IN THE MEADOW.

_____

_____

_____

C: Color Words

Think of colors that describe your topic. These might be colors you actually see when you look at your topic (a dog's BLACK fur, your friend's GREEN eyes), or colors that remind you of your topic or the way you feel about it (your friend's BLUE mood or HOT PINK personality). Try to use words that tell a picture. Use fancy words (auburn, silver, golden, jet-black) as well as simple words (red, yellow, blue).

List as many colors as you can. If you can't fill all six lines, repeat the colors you like best.

_____   _____   _____

_____   _____   _____

Playing PoemBuilder

Using the word list(s) your teacher will give you and a single die (half of a pair of dice), you will start building your poem. The die will help you to determine the number of words in each line, then the different categories of words (S for Senses, E for Emotions, N for Naming, A for Action— C for Color comes later), and finally a specific word within each category. You will enter your words on a PoemBuilder Chart, then use them to create the first rough draft of your poem.

PoemBuilder

A filled-in sample chart is found on page 63. You may want to look it over to get an idea of how your own chart will turn out.

You'll need to keep these pages in front of you: your word list(s) and your PoemBuilder Chart. Your teacher will give you a blank chart.

Step 1: Determining the Number of Words on Each Line

Your poem will be 6 lines long. How many words will be on each line? If you look at the PoemBuilder Chart, you'll see that you can have anywhere from 1-6 words per line.

Roll the die 6 times to determine how many words you'll have on each line. Write the numbers you roll in the far left column of your PoemBuilder Chart.

If you look at the sample chart on page 63, you'll see that the first number rolled was a 3. This means that the first line of the poem will have 3 words. Notice that the boxes under "Word 4," "Word 5," and "Word 6" have been crossed out. As you roll the die, cross out the boxes you won't be filling in on your PoemBuilder Chart. (If you roll a 6, you'll be filling in all 6 boxes. If you roll a 1, cross out 5 boxes.)

Roll again if...

...you roll the same number for more than two lines in a row (unless you want a repeated effect),

...you roll a 1 more than once, and

...you roll a 6 more than once.

Step 2: Determining the Word Categories

Which categories will your words come from? Notice that the boxes in the "Words and Word Categories" columns all contain the phrase, "from Group ___." To fill in the blanks, just roll the die.

If you roll this number:	*write this letter in the blank:*
1	S (for Senses)
2	E (for Emotions)
3 or 4	N (for Naming)
5 or 6	A (for Action)

If you look at the sample chart on page 63, you'll see that the first word in the first line will come from the S category. So will the second word in the first line. The third word in the first line will come from the E category. There won't be any fourth, fifth, and sixth words in this line; those spaces have been crossed out.

Keep rolling the die to fill in the blanks on your PoemBuilder Chart.

Roll again if...

...you roll the same number more than twice in a row (unless you want a repeated effect).

Step 3: Choosing Your Words

Now that you know which categories your words will come from, how will you decide which words to use? By rolling the die!

If you look at your word list, you'll see that the synonyms beside each main word are numbered from 1-6. These numbers correspond to rolls of the die. Let's say that you're using the Beginning Word List, and you checked BIG in the S category. If you now roll a 6, you might decide to use "big" as the first word in the first line of your poem. Write it in the box on your PoemBuilder Chart. (See the sample chart on page 63.)

Of course, you also checked other words in the S category. This means that you get to *choose* which words you want to use. If you roll a 6, and if you checked SMELLS GOOD, you might decide to use "nose treat" as your first word(s) instead of "big." If you checked SOUNDS PRETTY, you might choose to use "melodious." It's up to you.

You only have choices for the S and E categories. For the N and A categories, you must write the word that matches the number you roll on the die.

Keep rolling the die to fill in the boxes on your PoemBuilder Chart.

Roll again if...

...you really don't like the results of your first roll.

Writing Your First Rough Draft

Copy the words from your PoemBuilder Chart onto a piece of paper. Keep the words on each line together. If you don't like the way a line or a set of words turns out, roll the die to find new words. However, you don't have to like every line right away in order to continue. Soon you'll be revising and polishing this draft into an excellent finished poem.

SAMPLE POEMBUILDER CHART

This sample chart is for a short poem of four lines. The rough draft and the final revised and polished poem are shown on the next page.

Lines of poetry Number of words per line	Words and Word Categories					
	Word 1	Word 2	Word 3	Word 4	Word 5	Word 6
1. _3_	from Group_S_ Big	from Group_S_ Smelling	from Group_E_ Colorful (red?)	from Group_	from Group_	from Group_
2. _1_	from Group_S_ Nice to touch	from Group_	from Group_	from Group_	from Group_	from Group_
3. _2_	from Group_A_ Being happy	from Group_N_ Skate- board	from Group_	from Group_	from Group_	from Group_
4. _2_	from Group_E_ Colorful	from Group_N_ Dream	from Group_	from Group_	from Group_	from Group_

First Rough Draft

Big, smelling colorful
nice to touch
being happy skateboard
colorful dream

Revised and Polished Final Poem

The writer added ideas, changed words, and changed the order and position of words.

MY SKATEBOARD

My board smells like red cedar bark—
and is smooth as baby's skin!
A colorful board—fun to touch and ride,
races like a dream across ramps...
Skateboarding through the air my greatest thrill!

Revising and Polishing Your Poem

After determining all of the words for your poem and writing them down, read your first rough draft. You can now rewrite your poem to say exactly what you want it to say. Follow these steps:

1. Go over your PoemBuilder poem and underline or circle the phrases you like best.

2. Cross out any words or lines that don't make sense.

3. Add words to make your lines stronger.

4. Add any new thoughts, words, or ideas that come to you.

5. Change the order of the words and/or lines.

You may want to consider one or more of these additional changes:

6. Make words rhyme.

7. Change words by adding "-ing" or "'s."

8. Use creative capitalization.

9. Use creative punctuation—add commas, dashes (—), ellipses (...), periods, question marks, exclamation points, colons, etc.

Sample PoemBuilder Poems

See how PoemBuilder helped these three students to write powerful poems.

MY BOZO BOY
by Sherry Anderson

Original PoemBuilder	Rewrite	Final Poem
(About a boyfriend named Phillip, nickname: Bozo)		
Bozo boy nice to touch	Bozo ^{is} ^ boy nice to touch	*Bozo boy is nice to touch*
lover boy baby boy	lover boy ^ baby boy	*Lover boy—my baby boy.*
Good taste smells good blue	~~Good taste smells good blue~~	*Phillip loves me so*
small loves me Phillip	^{Phillip} ^ ~~small~~ loves me ^{so} ^ Phillip	*I love him in his turquoise clothes.*
quiet turquoise I love him	^{I love him in his} ^ quiet turquoise ^{clothes} ^ ~~I love him~~	
black bozo	~~black bozo~~	

MY TEACHER
by Mike Willitz

Original PoemBuilder	Rewrite	Final Poem
(About a teacher, Miss Smith)		
Serious Smithying built	*Serious Smith~~ying~~* ^{is} ^ *built* ^{with class} ^	*Serious Miss Smith is built with class*
old-fashioned pretty-sounding mouth treat	^{She is} ^ *old-fashioned* ^{and} ^ *pretty-sounding* ~~mouth treat~~	*she is old-fashioned and pretty-sounding,*
Rainbowish modern colors lifelike	^{and dresses in} ^ *rainbowish modern colors* ~~lifelike~~	*and dresses beautifully in rainbowish modern colors.*

MY MICHELLE
By Wesly Jones

<u>Original PoemBuilder</u>	<u>Rewrite</u>	<u>Final Poem</u>
(About a friend named Micki)		
Huge dresses scorching lady's fashion	Micki with *~~Huge~~ ^ dresses ^ scorching lady's fashion*	*Micki dresses with* *scorching lady's fashion,*
Hot woman natural reds and whites	joyful fashion ^ *~~Hot woman natural reds~~* to me *~~and whites~~ ^*	*Joyful fashion to me!*
Micki quiet and soft fashion joyful	She is also *~~Micki~~ ^ quiet and soft ~~fashion~~* *~~joyful~~*	*She is also quiet and soft.*

Coming Up with a Title

Some poets start by writing a title. Others add a title when their poem is finished. You can make up a title now or when you're through revising and polishing—it's up to you.

A title can describe the poem or the subject, or it can be something completely different. A title can be funny or serious, quiet or attention-getting. For example, if I were writing a poem about my wife, Judy, I might title it "Judy" (her name), "My Best Friend" (what she means to me), or "Hey, Lifeguard, Throw Me a Valentine" (a humorous way to describe my feelings).

Write your title here: _____

Finishing Your Poem

Write or type a clean copy of your final revised and polished poem. Put the title at the top.

How does it feel to be a poet?

PART 2

Exciting Writing, Speaking and Reading

Introduction

he projects in Part 2 take you off of the written page to the speaker's podium and the stage, behind the story in a newsletter, and into the mind of a character in a book. Here you can explore what it is like to give a speech, be an actor, or write a skit. Most lessons begin with group warm-ups or games. Before you create and practice a speech, you'll be challenged to repeat tongue-twisters. You'll exercise your acting muscles by playing charades. You'll relax with a story from a book or magazine, film or video; then, instead of writing the usual report, you'll stretch your imagination with assignments that spotlight plot, character, and setting.

Home Assignment

This assignment is about your favorite "home"—in fact or in imagination. You'll brainstorm all kinds of ideas using drawings, words, and lists. You'll also reinforce what you learned in Part 1 about 4-Step Writing, with a new emphasis on opening and closing sentences.

Public Speaking

You'll start by developing beginning speech making skills. You'll learn some of the tricks professional speakers use to communicate with voice and gesture. Then you'll join the big leagues of speech making by writing a prepared speech of your own. As you'll discover, this is very similar to writing a composition, except that you rely more on an outline than complete sentences.

Theater Games and Script Writing

Do you enjoy watching movies? Would you like to try acting or writing a short skit? You'll learn some warm-ups that real actors use before going on stage or in front of the cameras. You'll also find out how people write plays. You'll develop a greater appreciation for drama so you can get more out of the movies, TV programs, and plays you see.

Publishing a Classroom Newsletter

Have you ever wondered what it would be like to be a reporter? Perhaps your class will have time to create a newsletter. As you'll see, you can write all kinds of articles for a newsletter, from surveys to interviews, music reviews, sports stories, fashion stories, even poetry.

Imaginative Literature and Story Assignments

After reading a story or watching one on TV, you'll describe the different elements in new and exciting ways. For example, instead of just telling about the main character, you'll imagine that he or she goes to your school, and you'll fill out a report card for the character. Instead of just telling about the setting and plot, you might create a travel poster about the setting or draw a cartoon showing the plot.

Home Assignment

ome people live in the same house or apartment for all or most of their lives. Others move from place to place. They may live in many different towns or cities, even different countries. When you look back on the places you have lived, which one did you like best and why? Remembering your favorite home can be a warm and satisfying experience. If you sit quietly and really think about it, you can build a skyscraper of memories. (NOTE: If you have always lived in the same place, think about another home you have visited often enough to have strong memories. For example, this might be your grandparents' home, a friend's home, or a neighbor's home. Or imagine a home you would like to live in someday.)

You can use your memories to build three powerful paragraphs about your favorite home. In this activity, you'll find that remembering (or imagining) your favorite home and drawing it, then writing about it follow similar steps.

Picture yourself sitting quietly somewhere and drawing the plans for your home. You start by listing the number of rooms and remembering important details about them. After fleshing out your memories, you make a rough sketch of the floor plan. In writing, this is similar to writing the first (rough) draft. You look over your plan and suddenly remember something you forgot to include. You revise and edit your house plans, just like you revise and edit an essay. At last you are ready to draw up your final plans—and to write your final draft.

Let's see how brainstorming, listing, drawing, roughing in, drafting, revising, and editing can meet and work together as you describe your favorite home. In this activity, you'll use your writing skills to describe in three paragraphs the most wonderful and memorable home you have ever lived in—whether in real life or your imagination.

Brainstorming Ideas and Identifying Your Style

Do you know your working or learning style? Do you like to work alone, doodle before you write, list ideas and write quickly, or let your ideas simmer for a while before starting to write? When you take time to experiment and figure out which style you prefer, you can use it again. As you generate ideas for the essay about your home, you'll try out a number of different styles using words, memories, lists, and drawings. Pay attention to which style works best for you. Then you can re-use that style for future projects.

The following questions will help you to start brainstorming. Beneath each question you'll find additional directions that will inspire more ideas. Soon the memories of your favorite home will turn from a trickle to a flood. Be sure to save all of your ideas.

But first: Visualize your topic. Picture your favorite home. This is a special place with special memories for you. You felt happy and comfortable there. Try to capture that feeling by getting comfortable now. If possible, play some relaxing music. Do a few stretches and take some deep breaths. Then write or draw your answers. If you write *and* draw, use separate sheets of paper for each—one for your written responses, one (or more) for your drawings. Number your answers and staple the pages together.

1. Was your favorite home large or small?

    ◆ Draw it the way you remember seeing it when you stood in front of it. This kind of drawing is called an "elevation."

    ◆ Or, instead of drawing, make a list of everything you would see if you were standing in front of it.

Here is an example of a simple elevation:

2. How many rooms did it have?

◆ Make a list of the different rooms and the purpose(s) of each one and/or the things you did there.

◆ Draw a sketch of your home showing the different rooms as if you were looking down on them. This kind of drawing is called a "floor plan." Add one or two details that are important to you for personal reasons. (Remember, this is only a sketch. You'll draw a more detailed floor plan later in this activity.)

Here is an example of a simple floor plan:

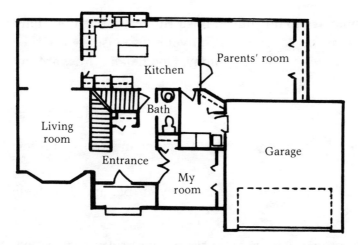

3. Which room was your favorite? Where did you have the best time?

◆ Draw a floor plan for the room that shows everything in it (as much as you can remember).

◆ Or make a list of the things in your favorite room.

4. Did you like the neighbors or other people who lived nearby? What were they like? Did you meet anybody special?

◆ Make a list of several words describing your neighbors. Circle the one word that seems to describe them best.

5. When you lived in your favorite home, did you go to school? What was the name of your school?

◆ Did you go to church, temple, or another place of worship? Draw it or make a list of the things you remember about it.

◆ Did you join a nearby club or organization? Make a drawing or a list describing what it was like and what you did.

◆ Did you play a sport at a nearby park or community center? Make a drawing or a list to describe your experience.

6. What things do you remember most clearly about your old neighborhood?

   ◆ What people do you remember most clearly? Draw or list some of the things you enjoyed doing with them.

7. On what kind of street was your favorite home located?

   ◆ Use words and pictures to show the sights, sounds, and smells you remember.

8. Of all the things you remember doing in your favorite home, which ones were the *most* fun?

   ◆ If possible, try to do your brainstorming for this question at home. Put on some music you enjoy. Print your responses, write them in cursive, use cut-out letters or calligraphy. Doodle and draw around the words. Decorate the entire page.

9. Did you have a special pet when you lived in your favorite home?

   ◆ Draw your pet, or draw something you and your pet often did together.

   ◆ Or make a list of words describing your pet and your feelings about your pet.

10. What other special memories do you have of this place? Draw, doodle, or list your thoughts about...

    ◆ the weather
    ◆ certain foods, clothing, music, holidays
    ◆ the room you slept in
    ◆ the places you visited

    ◆ conversations
    ◆ sounds
    ◆ surprises
    ◆ the way your family acted

After you have finished brainstorming, take a moment to think about your favorite style. How does your brain work best? We all have our own preferred style (or styles) of thinking, remembering, and being creative. Read the following list and check whatever method sparks the most ideas in your mind. You may check more than one.

☐ writing sentences   ☐ writing words
☐ drawing pictures   ☐ making lists
☐ doodling   ☐ asking questions
☐ listening to music   ☐ talking to other people

Drawing the Floor Plan

On a separate sheet of paper, draw a floor plan of your favorite home showing all of the rooms. You have just done quite a bit of brainstorming about this place, so you should have several details to consider. Use as many as possible in your drawing. Be sure to include a lot of details in your favorite room. These might be a combination of drawings, labels, and notes.

Your floor plan might start out looking something like the following, but you'll want to add even more details.

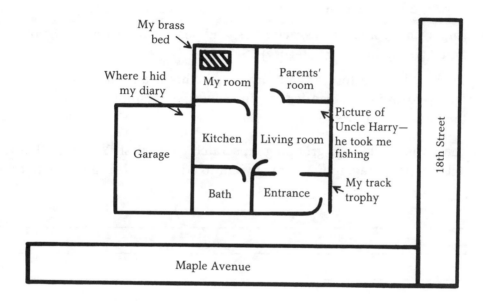

Writing Your Essay

You've just finished a drawing from memory about your favorite home. Now it's time to write an essay that describes your home in words. Start by reviewing your brainstormed ideas (written and drawn). Then follow the 4-Step Writing process outlined next. These steps become your "floor plan" for writing your essay.

If you compare this 4-Step Writing process to the one you learned in Part 1 of *Exciting Writing*, you'll notice some differences (although the four main steps are the same). As you continue to use 4-Step Writing over the next several months (and years), you may want to make additional changes to fit the requirements of what you are writing—and to suit your personal style.

Your final essay will be three paragraphs long. You'll probably be able to use all or most of your ideas in your essay.

Step 1: Prewriting
(Brainstorming and Organizing Ideas)

Start by reviewing your ideas (written and drawn) from the brainstorming activity. Next, group your most important ideas together for possible paragraphs. Some groups you might want to consider are:

◆ My favorite rooms (group ideas for each room)

◆ Things I did in each room (group ideas for each room)

◆ Memories from each room (group ideas for each room)

◆ How the home and neighborhood changed over time (group ideas by time)

◆ Important people, places, activities, and possessions from my favorite home (group ideas by category)

◆ Things I'll never forget about my favorite home and that time of my life (group ideas into categories of your choosing. Examples: pets, neighbors, hobbies, school, friends, etc.)

You may want to do your grouping on scratch paper first. You'll need at least 4 to 6 ideas per paragraph. You may want to add new ideas and delete others.

Ideas for the first paragraph:

_____

_____

_____

_____

_____

_____

_____

_____

_____

Ideas for the second paragraph:

_____

_____

_____

_____

_____

_____

_____

_____

_____

_____

Ideas for the third paragraph:

_____

_____

_____

_____

_____

_____

_____

_____

_____

_____

Now number the ideas for each paragraph. Decide which should go first, second, third, etc.

Step 2: Writing the First (Rough) Draft

On a separate sheet of paper, write (or type) your first draft as quickly as you can. Leave extra lines before and after each paragraph. You'll use these lines to add or change your opening and closing sentences.

Remember the four rules of first-draft writing:

RULE #1: Ignore Spelling

RULE #2: Skip Lines

RULE #3: Keep Writing

RULE #4: Don't Erase (just ~~cross out~~ words you don't want)

When you're finished with your rough draft, go back and make sure that each paragraph has an opening and a closing sentence. If you need help, study these hints and examples:

◆ An opening sentence:

— makes a general statement. Example: "This was the one home I felt I could always come back to, no matter how old I get."

— asks a question. Example: "What would it be like to revisit my secret hiding place from my childhood days?"

- gives important and interesting details. Example: "The outside was a basic gray, but inside that house was the warmth of a very lively family."

- takes an unusual twist; uses facts or humor. Example: "It wasn't like other homes—it was more like an asylum for wild and crazy humor."

As you add or revise each *opening* sentence, check it off:

☐ opening sentence for first paragraph done

☐ opening sentence for second paragraph done

☐ opening sentence for third paragraph done

◆ A closing sentence:

- restates the opening sentence, with different wording. Example: "I feel I can always come back here, at any age, for the rest of my life."

- uses signal words like "in conclusion," "for these reasons," "because of this," "in summary." Example: "In conclusion, this house will always be my favorite home." "For these reasons, I will never forget this place."

- states a final opinion or asks a question. Examples: "Some people think you can't ever revisit your past, but I disagree—it's great to go back in your mind." "I believe I'll still want to go back there when I'm 65." "How would you like to go back to your favorite place?"

As you add or revise each *closing* sentence, check it off:

☐ closing sentence for first paragraph done

☐ closing sentence for second paragraph done

☐ closing sentence for third paragraph done

Step 3: Revising the First Draft and Writing the Second Draft

Read your rough draft out loud to yourself. Listen to how it sounds and make changes to improve your essay. Then read it out loud to someone else. Ask questions:

◆ Which parts were most interesting?

◆ Did I leave anything out? Was anything unclear?

◆ Would you recommend changing anything?

If possible, read your essay out loud to your teacher and ask for feedback. Make any additional changes you think will improve your essay. Write a clean copy of your second draft.

Step 4: Editing for the Final Draft

Edit your second draft with **COPS**:

Capitalization

— Capitalize the first word in each sentence.

— Capitalize all proper nouns (names of businesses, schools, brand names, geographical areas, people's names, titles of books, songs, groups, or movies, the word "I," etc.)

Overall Appearance and Style (for the final draft)

— Keep your handwriting well-spaced and legible.

— Start with a clean piece of paper. Keep it neat (no smudges, tears, or extra marks)

— Use straight margins and indent the first sentence in each paragraph.

— Write a title on the top line.

Punctuation

— End each sentence with a . or ? or !

— Use commas when they are needed.

— Use complete sentences (subject and verb).

— Don't start sentences with "so," "but," "and," or "well."

Spelling

— Check words you often misspell.

— Circle any words you feel unsure about.

— Ask for help or look up the words.

Now write your final draft—in ink, on a typewriter, or with a word processor—and turn it in.

Public Speaking

Getting Started

hroughout your life, you may have many opportunities to give speeches. Occasionally you might be asked to speak to hundreds of people, but more likely—and more often—you will speak to only a few. If you work in sales, you will give your "speeches" to one or more customers at a time. If your job involves greeting people, leading tours, answering phones, asking questions, teaching, or giving directions, you will be speaking to groups or individuals for most of every day.

Even if you have never given a speech, it isn't as hard or as scary as you might believe. If you think of short speeches as verbal paragraphs, and longer speeches as essays, it quickly becomes clear that you already know quite a bit about public speaking.

There is one big difference between writing and speaking. In writing, grammar counts a lot, but in speaking, the way you use your eyes, voice, hands, and face is more important. When you speak, your gestures and your voice become your grammar and punctuation. You're about to learn different ways to enhance your communication skills by using expressions, body language, and even made-up sounds.

In the first part of this lesson, you'll practice becoming more expressive. The speeches you create won't require much planning, and you won't have to memorize anything. In the second part, you'll write an original speech and deliver it before an audience. Read on...and then speak on.

Voice: Clarity Warm-Ups

"Could you repeat that please?"

How many times have you had to ask people to repeat something they just said because their speech was unclear or not loud enough? Perhaps you have been asked to speak more clearly or speak up. We all get lazy and mush-mouthed at times.

Have you ever been frustrated at a movie or a play because you couldn't hear what the actors were saying, or you could hear their voices but not understand the words? Actors and speakers must learn to speak clearly—with clarity. The following games will help you to speak with greater clarity.

Say Hello

Before you can speak more clearly, you first have to tune up your ears so you can really hear yourself and others. This is a warm-up game actors use. By playing it, you'll learn to listen more carefully to voices.

You'll need a blindfold. Here are the rules:

1. One player puts on the blindfold.

2. Everyone else stands behind the blindfolded player. They take turns saying their names and the word "Hello." (Example: "Marvin Nelson. Hello.") The blindfolded player listens carefully.

3. Now everyone but the blindfolded player moves to a new position. They take turns saying "hello" again—but *without* giving their names, and in a different order from the first time. In between, the blindfolded player tries to guess who is speaking.

4. Another player puts on the blindfold and the game begins again.

Breathing and Speaking Games

Good speakers are loud and clear because they are able to control their breath and mouth when speaking. In these three games, you'll learn how to use and control your breathing in different ways. You'll learn how to use your tongue, lips, and breath as you practice slow and fast talking.

Your group will need a passage (two to three paragraphs) from a book that is easy to read (fairly simple vocabulary, uncomplicated sentences). Give everyone a chance to read it out loud before you start playing. Practice taking in deep breaths and letting them out as you read. You should find that you can speak with more volume and less effort if you concentrate on deep breathing while you speak.

You'll also need a stopwatch or a clock or watch with a second hand. Ask for volunteer timekeepers. For the Fast Talker game, ask for volunteer judges.

LONG-WINDED TALKER

See who can read the most words or lines in 15 seconds without taking a breath. (Tip: Start by taking a big breath, then let it out slowly as you read, as if you were underwater.) If you don't know a word, skip it. When 15 seconds are up, count the words or lines.

FAST TALKER

For this game, you are allowed to take in quick breaths. See how many lines you can read in one minute. (Tip: Move your lips a lot and breathe only a few times.) You earn a point for each line you start; you lose a point for each word the judge can't hear or understand.

SLOW TALKER

See who can read the fewest words or lines in 15 seconds without taking a breath. You can't pause between words, and one word must lead into the next. In other words, you must read in slow motion. If you pause, you must stop. When 15 seconds are up, count the words or lines.

Clarity Games

If your lips get lazy, your words come out softly and mushy. To get around this, speakers and actors use lip warm-up exercises. You can try these exercises to exercise your lips and mouth before giving a speech.

LOOSE LIPS

Certain letters, sounds, and words require more lip effort than others. Can you guess which ones? Move your lips as much as possible while pronouncing these letters and letter combinations out loud.

B   P   T   LL   ER   ST   NST   SK   SH   ING   S   D

Now try these words. Remember to use deep breathing.

Told	**Bit**
Tell	**Sing**
Tall	**Shop**
Pit	**Scope**
Sit	

Try these words next. See how quickly and clearly you can pronounce each one. Exaggerate the underlined letters and letter combinations.

◆   Words with beginning sound emphasis:

<u>sch</u>ool	<u>sh</u>allow
<u>sk</u>ill	<u>sh</u>ip
<u>sc</u>ale	<u>sh</u>ale

◆ Words with ending sound emphasis:

again<u>st</u>	shelve<u>s</u>
mu<u>st</u>	dea<u>d</u>
ju<u>st</u>	fire<u>d</u>
goi<u>ng</u>	stoppe<u>d</u>
flowi<u>ng</u>	teena<u>ger</u>
saili<u>ng</u>	screwdriv<u>er</u>
sail<u>s</u>	believ<u>er</u>
birth<u>s</u>	

TONGUE-TWISTERS

Now for the real challenge: tongue-twisters! Follow these steps as you practice each one.

1. Read it silently to yourself.
2. Read it silently and move your lips without making any sounds.
3. Read it slowly out loud.
4. Read it faster and faster out loud.

Rubber baby buggy bumpers.

Red leather, yellow leather.

He sawed six slender, slippery, silver saplings.

A swan swam over the swell. Swim, swan, swim!

A tree toad loved a she-toad
that lived up in a tree.
He was a three-toed tree toad,
but a two-toed toad was she.
The three-toed tree toad
tried to win the she-toad's heart.
But when two-toed met three-toed,
one toe kept two toads apart.

Voice: Tone Tune-Ups

Has there ever been a time when you asked someone for a favor, the person said "no," and you went back later and asked again? Probably—if you felt that the first "no" was not very serious. How could you tell? Because there are many different ways to say the word "no." Depending on how it is said and the speaker's tone of voice, this one short and simple word can mean at least eight different things:

1. "Absolutely not!"
2. "I'm too tired to think about it right now."
3. "Don't make me laugh."
4. "I don't think so, but maybe."
5. "Okay—if you ask again, and if you ask in the right way."
6. "We'll see."
7. "I don't have enough information to give you a yes answer."
8. "I'm busy. Go away."

If you asked your parents for money and they said "no," which "no" would it be? Can you say the word "no" in the eight ways given? Can you think of other ways that aren't on the list?

A good speaker can take any word and give it a different meaning, depending on how it is said. In this lesson, you'll practice using your tone of voice to communicate meaning.

Oh, No!

You are ten minutes late to class. The teacher asks you why you're late and you give a great excuse—something like "my locker was jammed." The teacher responds with one word: "Oh."

How many different ways could the teacher say "oh"? Look at the chart on the following page and circle the way your favorite teacher might say "oh."

Teacher says:	Teacher means:
1. "Oh."	*Skeptical/doubtful:* "I don't believe you. Go get a pass."
2. "Oh."	*Approving:* "That's the best excuse I've ever heard! You win the prize!"
3. "Oh."	*Sarcastic:* "I hope that coming to class isn't too much trouble for you."
4. "Oh."	*Hurt:* "I can't believe you keep doing this. When you're late to class and barge in during my lecture, you interrupt me and disrupt the class."
5. "Oh."	*Angry:* "Do you really expect me to believe that?"
6. "Oh."	*Silly:* "Watch out—a spitball is coming your way!"
7. "Oh."	*Very angry:* "So you thought you'd get away with it, right? That's two hours' detention for you, starting today."
8. "Oh."	*Feeling ill:* "I can't handle one more problem today."

Find a partner and act out the different ways to say "oh." Invent other ways and definitions. Take turns being the teacher and the student. Make up new reasons for not coming to class on time.

Student: "I'm late because _____

_____

_____."

Teacher: "Oh." (Meaning: _____

_____

_____.)

Different Tones

Pick a tone of voice to use when you say these words: "I promise to be on time tomorrow." Check your choice.

☐ tired   ☐ happy   ☐ busy

☐ excited   ☐ serious   ☐ don't believe it

☐ angry   ☐ funny   ☐ anxious

☐ bored   ☐ depressed   ☐ sorry

See if the others can guess your meaning from your tone of voice.

Gesture Games

A good speaker knows that words alone are not enough to make a speech interesting. Think about it: Would you enjoy talking with someone who stood perfectly still and never changed the way he or she looked, never moved an inch? A good speaker uses gestures to liven up the speech. In these exercises, you'll learn to communicate with gestures.

There are times when gestures and other body movements are just as useful as words or even more useful. People who are deaf or hearing impaired speak in sign language. Mimes tell stories without ever speaking. How would you ask someone for directions if you visited another country and couldn't find someone who spoke your language? These and other forms of communication rely on gesture.

Question Charades

The object of this game is to ask questions without using words—and make yourself understood. You'll need a stopwatch or a clock or watch with a second hand.

Imagine that you have just arrived in another country on a two-week vacation. So far, you haven't met anyone who understands you when you speak. But you want to ask these questions:

> *"Where can I find a place to eat?"*
> *"Is there a water fountain nearby?"*
> *"Where can I buy a jacket like yours?"*
> *"Would you like to go out with me tomorrow?"*
> *"Where is the bathroom?"*
> *"Does a bus or taxi come by here?"*

How could you communicate these questions without speaking? What gestures could you use?

To play Question Charades, divide into two teams of equal number. Each team writes one question for each member of the other team. (Example: If the other team has eight members, your team writes eight questions.) Write questions that a traveler in a foreign country might ask. When your team has finished writing questions, fold them in half or quarters and put them into a hat (or box) for the other team. Each player will draw one question in turn.

When you draw a question, you must act it out for your team. They have one minute to guess each question. They don't have to guess the exact words—just enough to know what you are asking. Time how long it takes each team to answer all of its questions. The team with the shortest total time wins the game.

◆ Remember to communicate only with gestures—no words.

◆ Help your team by using signals. (Make sure that everyone understands what they mean.) For example, bringing your thumb and index finger close together without touching means "You're close—try another, similar idea." Waving your hand means "No, wrong idea—forget this. Let me start over."

Adding Gestures to Words

Good speakers don't stand there like statues or stiff, expressionless boards. They smile, look at the audience, and gesture. This game gives you practice in adding gestures to words—with a twist: You'll begin by adding them to *someone else's* words, not your own. Start by choosing a partner. Then, when you're ready to play....

1. Pick two quotations from this list. Check your choices.

    ☐ "Join the army today! Please step forward now if you want to join."

    ☐ "You—yes, you, my fellow citizen—come here and listen. You can become as great as this land we live in."

    ☐ "Look over there at the red luxury car. What is it worth? Who will bid one, two, or even three dollars for this brand new car?"

    ☐ "Are you hiding? I can't see you! Where are you, Father? Mother, are you home?"

    ☐ "I will go no more! Here I stop—I can't take another step. I feel like I am slowly sinking...."

    ☐ "One point, and one point only do I wish to make today. So please listen carefully. I could save you a lot of money."

    ☐ "Listen to me. You just sit there and ignore me. It's like you're day-dreaming. Now sit up and listen!"

    ☐ "I have lost everything. I am finished, washed up. I guess there's nothing left to do but say good-bye and move to another town."

    ☐ "What did he look like? Was he tall? Did he weigh a lot? Was there a small scar on his cheek? How did he walk?"

    ☐ "You should have seen her. Very tall, with very muscular arms and legs...and very beautiful. And oh, how she smiled! She would knock you out with her smile."

2. Next, one partner reads the first quotation *without making any movements or gestures.* Stand absolutely still. Meanwhile, the other partner makes gestures that go with the quotation. It isn't necessary to act out each word—just the general mood or idea. *Variation:* Add humor. Have the gestures come "too late" or make them the opposite of the words being read.

3. Trade roles for the second quotation.

4. End by reading your own quotation and adding gestures while you read.

Remember to add a little gesture to your life as you speak to others.

Three Beginning Speeches

The speeches in this section let you practice all of the speech-making skills you have learned so far: breathing, clarity, tone of voice, and gestures. You will be rated on your performance. Your teacher will give everyone a copy of the Speaker Rating Form, but you will be rated by only three people: you, your teacher, and another student of your choice. Study the form so you know what you will be rated on and how to use the form when you are asked to rate someone else.

Speech #1: Reading a Passage

For this speech, you'll read a passage from a book, magazine, poem, album cover (record, cassette, compact disc), or advertisement. It should be something you enjoy reading. Before you read your passage to an audience, get to know it well and practice reading it out loud. Follow these steps in your practice. Do steps 2 through 5 in front of a mirror.

1. Underline any special words or phrases you want to emphasize with voice or gesture.

2. Read the passage again and again until you have memorized it or almost memorized it. This makes it easier to read to an audience.

3. Look up every so often as you read. Use your finger as a marker.

4. On special words, stop, pause, and look around. This adds drama to your reading.

5. Hold the book (or whatever you are reading from) high enough so that when you look down at the words your face is not lost and your voice is not buried. (But don't hold it so high that you hide your face and trap your voice.)

6. When you finish reading, don't race off. Pause and look up. This puts a polished finish on your reading.

When you are ready to give your speech, do it in this order:

    I.   INTRODUCTION: State the title or source of your passage and the author, if known.

   II.   BODY: Read the passage.

  III. CONCLUSION: Thank the audience and ask if there are any questions. Answer the questions.

Speech #2: Introducing Another Person

For this speech, you'll choose a partner and introduce that person to the class as though he or she were a total stranger to all of you. This might be your teacher or a classmate. If you choose someone you don't already know very well, preparing your speech will be more interesting for you. Follow these steps in your preparation.

1. Interview your partner to find out facts you can tell the audience. Ask questions like the following. Write down your partner's answers.

    a. What is your favorite food, music, sport, clothes, car, movie, TV show, etc.?

    b. Describe your family. Who is in it? What is each person especially good at doing?

    c. What do you do for fun in your spare time?

    d. Do you have any jobs or home responsibilities? Do you do volunteer work? Are you involved in clubs, sports, or other organizations?

    e. What do you hope to do with your life when you graduate from high school? Do you plan to go to college? What kind of job or career would you like to pursue?

    f. What is the most interesting place you have been to?

    g. If you could change one thing about school, or your life, or the world, what would it be?

2. Review the facts about your partner's life and circle the 5 to 8 most interesting ones. Put them in order from most important to least important.

3. Organize and write a speech outline. You will follow your outline when giving your speech. Use the ideas shown in [brackets] below. If you like, and if they fit your speech, you can use some of the words in the examples.

I.   INTRODUCTION

[Tell who you will talk about. State one thing that expresses your feelings about the person.]

Today I want to talk about <u>Alex Tamkin</u> *(name)*.

If I had to describe him in one word, it would be <u>creative</u>.

II. BODY

[State 5 to 8 interesting facts about the person. Begin and end with the two most interesting facts. This gives the audience something to think about at the beginning and end.]

A.   *Alex came to this country from Russia.*

B.   *He likes to write, play pool, and go to the movies in Old Town, Portland.*

C.   *Alex also enjoys painting. He learned it from his father, who was a painter and a woodworker.*

D.   *Alex's favorite movie is* <u>Gone with the Wind</u>.

E.   *Here's something you may not know about Alex: One of his plays was performed live in New York City.*

III. CONCLUSION.

[As you did in the Introduction, state one thing that expresses your feelings about the person. Three different examples are given here.]

In conclusion, I'd like to say:

1.   *I enjoyed learning about Alex because he is a creative guy.*

2.   *I think the fact that Alex is from Russia makes him very unique.*

3.   *Alex is a lot like me because we both like to write and paint. I enjoyed talking with him.*

Speech #3: Acceptance Speech

Sometime in your life you will be given a compliment, award, honor, trophy, prize, a toast at dinner, or a diploma. You may be called upon to "say a few words." This is called an acceptance speech. You don't have to prepare for it—you may not even know about it ahead of time, especially if you are surprised by an award—but you do need to include a few things in your speech. For example, you should always mention the people who are giving you the award, honor, etc. You should mention other people who have helped you along the way. Follow these steps to prepare a basic acceptance speech.

1.   Decide what you will be accepting. This can be an actual or made-up award, honor, prize, etc. It might relate to one of these categories. Check your choice:

☐   self-improvement   ☐   saving a life

☐   grades or school work   ☐   helping the environment

☐   sports   ☐   doing chores at home

☐   work performance   ☐   other: _____
    or experience   _____

☐   helping others   _____

2.   Decide who will be giving you the award, honor, prize, etc. (A person? An organization? Your school? Your club? Your parents?) Write the name here:

_____.

3.   Decide what your award is called. Is there any writing on it? What does it say? ("World's Greatest First-Base Coach?" "Hero/Heroine"? "First Prize for Cleanest Locker"? "Best Babysitter"? "Honor Roll Student"?) Write the words here: _____.

4.   Outline your speech. Write your outline on a note card you can refer to as you give your speech. Your outline should include these three parts:

I.   INTRODUCTION. Thank the people/organization for giving you the award. Mention the award by name.

II. BODY. Mention something about the people/organization giving you the award. Mention people who helped you along the way or made it possible for you to receive the award. Tell what the award means to you.

III. CONCLUSION. Thank again the people/organization giving you the award.

Preparing and Giving a Speech

In the first part of this lesson, you learned the basics of speech making, including using your voice and gestures to give your speeches impact. In this part, you'll write an original speech and give it in front of an audience. You'll start by creating an outline that will help to make your speech lively and exciting.

Organizing a speech is like organizing a short composition. You begin by making a list of items and ideas you want to include, then put them in order. The outline method you'll learn here is simple and effective. All you have to do is add examples and think of ways to make your speech interesting.

Don't forget the skills you learned in the first part of this lesson. Dazzle your audience with clarity, volume, gestures, and eye contact. Excite them with a speech they won't forget!

A Proven Speech Outline

Over the years, many books have been written about how to make speeches. The outline shown below is one of the best ways to organize a speech. It has been tested countless times and proven to work, so you can count on it to work for you. On the pages that follow, you'll see specific examples of this outline in action.

I.   INTRODUCTION

  A. Introduce yourself and state your topic.

  B. Capture your audience's attention.

   1. Ask a question.

   2. Use a prop to make a point.

   3. Tell a short story or anecdote to support or illustrate your point of view.

  C. State your main beliefs about the topic. State your position.

  D. Preview what you'll cover next.

II. BODY

Give 4 to 6 examples to prove your point. Organize your examples from most to least important, or from general to specific.

    A. (Example)

    B. (Example)

    C. (Example)

    D. (Example)

III. CONCLUSION

    A. Restate something important you said in the introduction.

    B. Ask your audience to carry out an action related to your topic.

Writing Your Outline

Suppose you had to make a speech about cigarette smoking. Are you for or against it? Should the rules about smoking in your school be changed? You're about to find out how a speech outline can take shape around this smoky topic.

The examples in this section are from a speech *against* smoking. You may have a different point of view about smoking, or you may be against smoking for different reasons than the ones included here. Read the examples before you start writing. You can use some of the ideas from the examples, but you must put them in your own words and add at least one new idea of your own.

The two main steps in speech writing are brainstorming and writing. They should be done in order, one at a time. Study the instructions and examples before you start writing.

Step 1: Brainstorm a list of ideas about your topic

Write your ideas on a separate sheet of paper. First, copy the <u>underlined</u> words. Then replace the words in *italics* with your own words. When you're done, you'll have a list of ideas to use in your speech outline.

<u>1. Topic</u>

Write your topic across the top of a piece of paper.

<u>"Speech Brainstorm: Against Smoking"</u>

If you have a different point of view about smoking, change the wording of the topic.

<u>2. My Three Reasons</u>

Under your topic, list three reasons why you feel strongly about it.

Examples:

    a.   I'd look dumb if I smoked.

    b.   Smoking would get me in trouble.

    c.   Smoking costs too much.

3.   <u>How the Audience Might Feel</u>

Think about your audience. List three reasons why your topic might appeal to them.

Examples:

    a.   Other people's smoking is bad for my health.

    b.   When I'm eating in a restaurant and someone next to me is smoking, it ruins my meal.

    c.   Smoking raises the costs of health care.

Step 2: Write the outline for your speech

Now you'll need to turn your brainstormed ideas into an outline. The following example shows you how to do this, one step at a time. Write your outline on a separate sheet of paper. Like you did for brainstorming, start by copying the <u>underlined</u> words. Then replace the words in *italics* with your own words. When you're through, you'll have a complete speech outline.

I.   <u>INTRODUCTION</u>

    A. <u>Introduce yourself and state your topic.</u>

    Example: My name is Joe Bloe. I am here to talk about the dangers and problems of smoking.

    B. <u>Capture your audience's attention.</u>

        1. <u>Ask a question.</u>

        The question should make your audience think about your topic.

        Examples:

        ◆ *Did you know that smoking 20 cigarettes will shorten your life by 120 minutes?*

        ◆ *How much will it cost you to smoke if you have to retire early because of lung cancer?*

        2. <u>Use a prop to make a point.</u>

        Examples:

        ◆ *Hold up a nail and say, "We pound nails in a coffin lid, and each time you smoke it's like pounding a nail into your own coffin lid."*

◆ *Pick up a tee shirt and sniff it while making a face. Turn to the audience and say, "This shirt was worn by a smoker. Would you want to sit next to this smell on a bus?"*

3. Tell a short story or anecdote to support or illustrate your point of view.

Examples:

◆ *When I was five years old, a house in our neighborhood burned to the ground. The fire was started by a smoker who fell asleep with a lit cigarette in his hand.*

◆ *My grandmother spends every day hooked up to an oxygen machine. She has emphysema. Before she got sick, she smoked two packs of cigarettes every day.*

◆ *My uncle died of lung cancer. I had to visit him during the last four weeks of his life, when he was undergoing chemotherapy. Let me tell you what it was like....*

C. State your main beliefs about the topic. State your position.

Example:

I believe smoking should be banned or more heavily taxed.

D. Preview what you'll cover next.

(Don't write this part yet. Wait until after you outline the body of your speech.)

Example:

I will talk about the health hazards of smoking, how it ruins social events like eating in restaurants, and why it costs taxpayers money.

II. BODY

Give 4 to 6 examples to prove your point. Organize your examples from most to least important, or from general to specific.

Example:

A. *The health hazards of smoking are many. Smoking is addictive. For pregnant women, smoking can cause birth defects. And everyone knows it can cause lung cancer.*

B. *And think back to the last time you went out to eat. You were in the middle of a great meal—only to have it ruined by smoking from another table. How many special events are ruined by other people smoking?*

C. *Finally, you and I pay the bill. When someone stops working due to lung cancer, they often have to go on some form of public assistance or use up insurance dollars. So who is paying the cost? You and I.*

(Go back and write your preview statement now. You know what will be in the body of your speech.)

III. <u>CONCLUSION</u>

    A. <u>Restate something important you said in the introduction.</u>

    Example:

    I am against smoking because each cigarette is like a nail in a coffin.

    B. <u>Ask your audience to carry out an action related to your topic.</u>

    Examples:

- *If you smoke, won't you please try to quit?*
- *Will you take the time to write to your congressperson about smoking?*
- *Will you donate time or money to the cancer society?*

My Speech Outline

Choose a new topic for your own speech. It should be a topic you feel strongly about and know something about (examples: school, privileges, students, young people, parents, rules, laws, families, employment, driving, curfews, etc.). You will use the same skills you practiced in the smoking speech to organize your speech.

Step 1: Brainstorm a list of ideas about your topic

1. Topic

Write your topic or title.

_____

2. My Three Reasons

List three reasons why you feel strongly about your topic.

    a. _____

    _____

    b. _____

    _____

    c. _____

    _____

3. How the Audience Might Feel

   List three reasons why your topic might appeal to them.

   a. _____

   _____

   b. _____

   _____

   c. _____

   _____

Step 2: Write the outline for your speech

Fill in the outline with ideas for your speech. Your ideas can come from written sources, people you talk to, TV programs, your own knowledge...anywhere. You don't have to write complete sentences. Use facts or phrases. If you need more room to write, add another page.

I. INTRODUCTION

   A. Introduce yourself and state your topic.

   _____

   _____

   _____

   _____

   _____

   B. Capture your audience's attention.

   1. Ask a question.

   _____

   _____

   2. Use a prop to make a point.

   _____

   _____

   3. Tell a short story or anecdote to support or illustrate your point of view.

   _____

   _____

   _____

   _____

   _____

_____

_____

_____

_____

_____

C. State your main beliefs about the topic. State your position.

_____

_____

_____

_____

_____

_____

D. Preview what you'll cover next. (Write this part after you outline the body of your speech.)

_____

_____

_____

_____

_____

_____

_____

_____

_____

_____

II. BODY

Give 4 to 6 examples to prove your point. Organize your examples from most to least important, or from general to specific.

A. The most important/most general idea:

_____

_____

B. The next most important or general idea:

_____

_____

C. _____

_____

D. _____

_____

E. _____

_____

F. The least important or most specific idea: _____

_____

III. CONCLUSION

A. Restate something important you said in the introduction.

_____

_____

_____

_____

B. Ask your audience to carry out an action related to your topic.

_____

_____

_____

_____

Working with Assigned Speech Topics

Here are two topics that are sure to challenge and excite you. Use all of the skills you have learned so far to outline your speech—and deliver it in front of an audience.

The Pet Peeve Speech

Think about something that really makes your blood boil. What annoys you? What is something you want to change? Is it the fact that you have to do certain things at certain times—like come home by 11:00 p.m. on the weekends, or finish doing the dishes by 7:00 at night, or turn off the TV by 10:00 p.m. on school nights, or limit your telephone calls to 10 minutes? Are you bugged by heavy traffic or having to wait in line? Is it the way some people treat other people? Do you have to use a product you hate? Are there rules you have to follow, even though you think they are totally unreasonable? Get fired up!

You'll probably use quite a few gestures during this speech. It can be a lot of fun to give.

The Sales Speech

Salespeople are called upon all the time to give speeches about their products. To prepare this kind of speech, you will need to add one more thing to your bag of speech-making tricks: demonstrating your "product."

Decide on a product you might like to sell. It should be something you are familiar with and could demonstrate or show with confidence and skill. Here are some examples. If any appeal to you, check your choice(s).

- ☐ clock radio
- ☐ camera
- ☐ watch or jewelry
- ☐ toy
- ☐ tool
- ☐ clothing
- ☐ small kitchen appliance

- ☐ sporting equipment
- ☐ cassette or compact disc
- ☐ cassette or compact disc player
- ☐ book or magazine
- ☐ something handmade
- ☐ candy or cookies
- ☐ video game

As you brainstorm ideas for your speech and start putting it together, consider the following questions and suggestions, adapted from a sales manual. Try to address as many as you can in your speech.

◆ Describe the company that makes the product.

What is their reputation? How long have they been in business? Is it a large company or a small company?

◆ What is the quality of the product?

Will it last? Can it be easily repaired? What materials are used to make it?

◆ What is the price and value of the product?

How does it compare to competitors' products? Can it be resold or traded in later? Will it increase in value over the years?

◆ What does the customer want and need? What is the customer looking for?

Ask some potential "customers." Tailor your responses to their needs.

◆ What are some other benefits of using the product?

◆ Is it easy for you to use the product? Will you be able to demonstrate it to your audience easily and quickly? Will demonstrating the product improve your speech?

Theater Games and Script Writing

efore actors go on stage or before the camera, they usually warm up their voices, bodies, and imaginations. One way to do this is by playing theater games with the other actors. Think of the games in this section as party games or pantomimes. Each starts with a question to engage your imagination. After thinking about the question, you follow the rules and suggestions. Use the follow-up questions if you want to go further. If there is time, your teacher might read the title, beginning questions, and rules and suggestions out loud and give a demonstration.

Six Theater Games

Grocery Bag

(A pantomime; acting without words)

Beginning Questions

What foods do you really enjoy or hate? Do your favorite (least favorite) foods come in boxes, bags, or cans? Are any of them hard to open, like potato chip bags? Suppose you went shopping and brought back a bag full of food. Imagine taking something out of the bag and eating it. Picture yourself opening the package, holding it, smelling it, and working with it (for example, do you eat it with your hands or a spoon? Do you eat it quickly or savor every bite?).

Game Rules/Situation to Act Out

1. Think of a food you love (or hate).

2. Take out a package. Show its size and weight by how you hold it.

3. Show how you get to the food. Do you peel it like a banana? Do you use your teeth to tear open the bag? Do you need a can opener?

4. As you eat the food, show what it tastes like or how it is eaten. Do you chew it a lot? Is it sticky? Does it have an aroma?

5. If the audience can't guess your food after four tries, repeat your actions, this time adding some sound effects.

Chores

(A pantomime with sound effects; acting without words)

Beginning Questions

What chores do you do at home? Which ones do you enjoy? Which ones do you hate? What materials or tools do you use? Do you make a face, like holding your nose when you take out the garbage? Do you make any sounds? Is the work itself noisy or quiet? Are you cheerful or grouchy while you are working?

Game Rules/Situation to Act Out

1. Choose a chore. Think about the materials you use. Think about the sound effects.

2. Show a chore you do, without speaking—but with sound effects.

3. If your chore involves going outdoors, show this. If you wear gloves or a hat while doing your chore, show this, too.

4. If you hate doing the chore, show this in your face and your actions.

5. If you get hot, wet, cold, or dirty, show this.

6. Complete the chore or continue until the audience guesses what you are doing.

Mirror, Mirror on the Wall...

(A partners game; observation and imitation)

Beginning Questions

What do you do when you first go to the mirror in the morning? What do you look at? What do you look for? What do you like to see—and what do you not like to see? Do you spend a lot of time in front of the mirror in the morning?

Game Rules/Situation to Act Out

1. Choose a partner—preferably someone you don't know very well, or someone who isn't a close friend.

2. Sit down facing each other.

3. One of you will be the actor, and the other will be the mirror, copying the actor's movements and actions as closely as possible. Decide who will be what.

4. (For the actor): Move your right hand slowly. Now move your left hand. Slowly move both hands...then nod.

5. (For the actor): It's morning; you just woke up. Go to the mirror and comb your hair.

6. Switch roles—the mirror becomes the actor, the actor becomes the mirror—and repeat steps 4 and 5.

7. (For the actor): Now you are putting on your clothes for school. You will have to stand for part of this performance. Do it slowly.

8. Switch roles and repeat step 7.

Seeing Eye

(A partners game of trust)

For this game, you will need to create a small obstacle course in the classroom. Introduce the game with the following description:

"If you take a walk with a friend who is blind, you may notice that your friend discreetly holds your elbow as you walk together. Meanwhile, it is your job to pay attention to your surroundings and describe them to your friend. For example, you might tell about obstacles in your path, such as a closed door, a desk, or a pile of books. You might need to tell your friend to turn sideways to move between a chair and the wall; to step up or step down; to duck; and so on. Your friend will have to trust you to give enough information—and the right kind of information—so he or she can walk safely. This game demonstrates that kind of communication and trust."

Beginning Questions

What would it be like to suddenly lose your sight? Would you have to trust other people more than you do now, or trust them in different ways? How would you get around at first?

Game Rules/Situation to Act Out

1. Choose a partner—preferably someone you know very little about.

2. Now imagine that you have suddenly lost your sight. (Close your eyes tight or put on a blindfold.)

3. Let your partner guide you through the obstacle course. Ask your partner to talk about and mention obstacles, steps, and special movements you must make.

4. Switch roles and repeat steps 1 through 3.

Walk That Walk

(Whole body movement without words)

Beginning Questions

Did you ever get trapped in mud? Mud up to your ankles? Mud up to your knees? How did you walk? In this game, you must show what happens as you walk across different kinds of terrain.

Write the following on individual slips of paper:

◆ barefoot walking across hot pavement

◆ very old and walking with a cane

◆ walking in knee-deep mud

◆ on a skateboard crossing a street

◆ in a wheelchair going down the hall

◆ walking across a cold and windy parking lot

◆ walking through piles of leaves

◆ underwater, walking along the ocean bottom

◆ walking across the surface of another planet, weighing three...times...as...much...as...you...do...now

◆ muscular, strong, strutting your stuff and showing off as you walk

◆ a baby taking your first steps

- walking across an icy pond

- a robot walking to the refrigerator to get an oil sandwich

Fold the slips of paper and put them in a hat or box. There should be one slip for each student. Invent more walks if needed.

Game Rules/Situation to Act Out

1. Everyone draws a slip of paper out of the hat or box and lines up along one side of the room.

2. One at a time, each person crosses to the other side, "walking the walk" described on his or her slip of paper. The others try to guess what the walker is doing. When someone guesses correctly, the walker returns to the line.

Tardy!

(Improvisation with words)

Beginning Questions

Some students try hard to please their teachers, and some do the opposite. How can you tell these students apart? How do they act differently?

Game Rules/Situation to Act Out

This game requires three actors—one to play the teacher, two to play the students. The rest of the class can play themselves.

The teacher has just started the lesson when two students walk into the room—tardy. One is the type who always tries to please the teacher. The other is the type who enjoys not pleasing teachers and/or feels picked on by teachers. Show how they behave when they walk in. What do they say? What do they do? What is their body language? What actions do they take? What are their facial expressions?

Related Situations to Improvise

Decide how many actors each situation will require. What type of person will each actor portray? What are the circumstances of each scene? (Examples: Parents are tired and grouchy at the end of a long day...or parents are relaxed and cheerful at the end of a long weekend.) Come up with details to make your scene more interesting.

- Asking parents for permission to....

- Asking the boss for a day off.

- Asking the coach about being able to play more.

- Asking the teacher if you can go to the restroom.

Script Writing: Dialogue, Stage Directions, Plot

Have you ever read a play? Have you ever acted in a school or community skit or play? Have you ever wished you could write the script? Now you can. *You* get to decide what the actors say and do.

First, you'll learn how to write dialogue. Later, you'll learn how to create a complete script, from beginning to end. Start by reading the skit that follows. It tells about Loren and his attempt to borrow money from his mother. As you read, consider these questions:

◆   Does this sound familiar?

◆   Does it sound realistic?

◆   Does it make sense?

Pay close attention while you read; there will be more questions at the end. Notice the script writing rules in the right-hand column.

TITLE: LOREN'S BIG NIGHT OUT????

Characters:

Loren Smith—a 16-year-old boy

Anne Smith—Loren's mother

Narrator

SCENE 1: THE QUESTION

Setting:

The living room of the Smith home.

Narrator:

It is 6:00 p.m. Loren eagerly waits for his mother to return home from work.

Script Writing Rules

1.   Write the title at the top. List the characters.

2.   Number each scene and give it a title.

3.   Describe the setting where the scene takes place.

Loren (muttering to himself):
I've got to get those tickets tonight, or it will be too late!

Narrator:
Loren's mother enters, takes off her coat, hangs it in the hall closet, sits in her favorite chair, and turns on the television to the evening news. Loren walks over in front of the TV and tries to get her attention.

Loren (politely, in a soft voice):
Mom, can I have an advance on my allowance tonight?

Mother (tired):
You've got to be kidding.

Loren (getting angry, his voice rising):
But I did all my chores!

Mother:
Don't you raise your voice to me.

Loren (begging):
I'm sorry....It's just that I promised....Oh, what's the use....

Mother (standing up and putting a hand on Loren's shoulder):
Let me think about it. I have a meeting tonight and I was just trying to relax for a few minutes. I had a hard day. We'll talk later, after I get home.
(Mother exits.)

Loren (sitting down and pouting):
How do I get myself into these situations?

4. Underline the characters' names. Start dialogue on the line below the name. Leave an extra line between characters.

5. Put stage directions in parentheses. Then the actors will know what you want them to do—without reading your stage directions out loud as part of the script.

Now answer these questions about "Loren's Big Night Out?????"

♦ Can you think of a better title for the skit?

♦ Does the playwright show that Loren's mother is tired? Yes or no? If yes, how?

♦ Do you think the dialogue is realistic? Why or why not?

♦ How might you change the ending or the beginning?

♦ Can you find two stage directions about emotions?

♦ Can you find two stage directions telling the actor what to do physically on stage?

Now rewrite the scene on a separate sheet of paper. Make at least four changes.

1. Change the title.

2. Change at least three stage directions.

3. Change at least three lines of dialogue.

4. Change the ending.

Writing Dialogue

1. Think back to a conversation you had recently. It might have been a friendly conversation or an argument. Maybe you were discussing a grade on a test or plans for the weekend. If you can't think of an interesting conversation you were involved in personally, consider writing one you overheard at school, in your neighborhood, at a bus stop, on a team, or in a mall.

2. Following the script writing rules on pages 105–106, write at least 7 to 10 lines of dialogue.

TITLE:

_____

_____

Characters:

_____

_____

_____

_____

SCENE NUMBER AND TITLE:

_____

_____

<u>Setting:</u>

_____

_____

_____

_____

DIALOGUE:

_____

_____

_____

_____

_____

_____

_____

_____

_____

_____

_____

_____

_____

_____

Comparing Real Life Dialogue to Dramatic Dialogue

Real life dialogue can sound so...dull. Dramatic skit dialogue is exciting, filled with questions, arguments, emotions, and humor. Which of the two scripts below is from real life, and which is from a dramatic play? How can you tell? Watch for clues while you read.

Script #1

George:

Hi, Tammy.

Tammy:

Hello, George.

George:

What a tough test that was in algebra today.

Tammy:

You can say that again.

George:

Do you think you passed?

Tammy:

Maybe. You?

George:

I hope so.

Script #2

Paul:

Marcy, can you believe the grades on this test?

Marcy:

I studied for hours and it doesn't even show.

Paul:

I notice the grades are in blue pencil.

Marcy:

That's odd. They're usually in red ink.

Paul:

Do you have an eraser?

Marcy:

What are you saying?

Paul:

My red pencil and your eraser could make the grading a bit more fair.

Now answer these questions about the two scripts:

1. Which script has the most interesting dialogue?

   ☐ Script #1 ☐ Script #2

2. Which script shows a character with a problem? Which script shows a character having to overcome an obstacle or problem in order to get what he or she wants—to reach a goal?

   ☐ Script #1 ☐ Script #2

3. What is the goal in script #2?

   Paul wants to _____

   _____

4. What obstacle or problem is Paul facing?

    Paul can't reach his goal unless _____

    _____

5. Which script shows conflict and has an ending?

    ☐ Script #1 ☐ Script #2

6. A script is boring if (check two):

    ☐ the character has a goal

    ☐ the character has no goal and just talks

    ☐ it ends after someone goes through a personal change or a change in his or her situation

    ☐ it simply ends when the character says the last line

7. Can you remember the last movie you saw that was boring or disappointing? What made it that way? Did it have any of the problems mentioned in question 6?

    The movie was boring or disappointing because _____

    _____

    _____

You're about to learn how to write interesting scripts in which the characters have goals, they face obstacles or problems, and the endings are interesting.

Planning Your Script

When you determine the main character's goal and the obstacles or problems he or she must overcome before reaching that goal, you're on your way to writing a good dramatic script. You must also carefully plan your ending. Playwrights call this "plotting the scene." Follow these four steps when plotting your scene or skit.

Step 1: Identify Your Main Character and State the Character's Goal

Your scene or skit must have a main character. Think about what this person will be like. Is your main character a male or a female? Is your main character older or younger than you? What does your main character look like? How is your main character like you, and unlike you? Describe your main character in only three lines:

_____

_____

_____

What is your main character's name? _____

Your main character must have a goal. He or she must want something very badly. What is something you want and might like to write about? New playwrights often write about their own goals and problems, or ones they are familiar with. What goal could you write about? Choose something from the list below or come up with your own idea.

☐   To change a grade on a test or paper

☐   To be yourself without giving into peer pressure
(example: dressing the way you want, listening to the music you like)

☐   To borrow the car or money for a date

☐   To help a friend who is in trouble

☐   To join a group or team that is hard to get into

☐   To solve a crime (example: a locker theft)

☐   Your own idea: _____

What is your main character's goal? _____

_____

_____

Step 2: State the Main Obstacle to the Goal

If your character simply reaches his or her goal without any effort, then your script will be boring. On the other hand, if your character has to be brave, sneaky, clever, or funny in order to reach the goal, or if he or she changes, suffers, or grows along the way, then your script will be interesting. Practice this dramatic technique by inventing an obstacle or problem for each goal described below. Sample obstacles are given to get you started.

Goal: The character needs money to go out on a date.

Sample obstacle: The money was supposed to be a reward for keeping his grades up, but he recently got a poor grade on a test.

Your obstacle: _____

_____

_____

Goal: The character wants to change a grade on a test or a paper.

Sample obstacle: She did not show up on test make-up day and the teacher is not thrilled.

Your obstacle: _____

_____

_____

Think about your main character. Think about his or her goal. What might get in the way? What problem might he or she confront? Who might try to prevent your character from reaching his or her goal?

What is the main obstacle to your character's goal? _____

_____

_____

Step 3: Add More Obstacles to Increase the Suspense

When you add more obstacles, you add more suspense—and you make your skit or scene longer. Suddenly your character is facing more than one problem—just as real people do in real life. It is during these difficult times that we learn the most about our character (and sometimes about ourselves).

Here is an example of what might happen when you add obstacles:

Goal: The character needs money to go out on a date.

Sample obstacle: The money was supposed to be a reward for keeping his grades up, but he recently got a poor grade on a test.

Another obstacle: He just found out that he has another test tomorrow, and he's not prepared. What will he say when his parents ask how his grades are going?

Another obstacle: A friend offers to help him get a good grade on tomorrow's test—by cheating. In return, the friend wants a ride to the game on Friday. Should the character go along?

Another obstacle: He has already made a date for Friday. If he can't get any money, he will have to cancel the date. This is someone he has wanted to ask out for a long time. He will be embarrassed—and maybe she won't want to make another date with him.

Add two more obstacles or problems for the character in this scene:

1. _____

_____

_____

2. _____

_____

_____

Create two more obstacles or problems for your main character:

1. _____

_____

_____

2. _____

_____

_____

Step 4: Plan Your Ending

There are at least three ways to end a scene. Read the descriptions and suggestions, then decide how you would end the scene about the character who needs money for a date. Write your own ending for practice.

1.   The character changes.

Suggestion: He decides to plan a date that won't cost any money. He calls his date and suggests that they go on a star-gazing walk organized by a local nature center. He tells her that it will be fun and interesting, and explains that the center will serve refreshments after the walk.

2.   Something new comes up.

Suggestion: He learns that his parents are planning a big party for Friday night. He offers to clean the house on Thursday if they will pay him to do it. Then he will have the money he needs for Friday.

3.   The main character exits and a new scene is added.

Suggestion: He argues with his parents and exits the scene. In the next scene, he comes back to them with a list of chores he could do to raise money by Friday. Or he calls a friend and asks to borrow money.

Your choice:

☐   ending 1

☐   ending 2

☐   ending 3

Or write your own ending to this scene: _____

_____

_____

_____

_____

Now write an ending to the scene involving your character: _____

_____

_____

_____

_____

Outlining Your Scene or Skit

You will use the techniques and steps you have learned so far to write an outline for an original scene or script. Follow the outline provided here. If you decide to stay with the character, goal, obstacles, and ending you developed in the preceding activities, you have already done much of what you need to do. Or, if you prefer, you can start over, or change any part of your outline as you come up with new ideas.

Step 1: Identify Your Main Character and State the Character's Goal

My main character's name: _____

A three-line description of my main character:

_____

_____

_____

My main character's goal: _____

_____

_____

_____

Other characters and brief descriptions:

Name: _____

Description: _____

_____

_____

_____

Name: _____

Description: _____

_____

_____

_____

Name: _____

Description: _____

_____

_____

_____

Step 2: State the Main Obstacle to the Goal

The main obstacle to my character's goal: _____

_____

_____

Step 3: Add More Obstacles to Increase the Suspense

Two more obstacles or problems for my main character:

1. _____

_____

_____

2. _____

_____

_____

Any more obstacles?

_____

_____

_____

_____

Step 4: Plan Your Ending

Choose one:

1. Here is how my main character changes: _____

_____

_____

_____

2. Something new that comes up: _____

_____

_____

_____

3. Here is how my main character exits and what happens in the next scene:

_____

_____

_____

Writing Your Scene or Script

Now turn your outline about characters, goals, obstacles, and endings into a script. Use a separate sheet (or sheets) of paper. Start by writing a rough draft, then show it to your teacher for feedback. Make changes, add more dialogue (and possibly more obstacles), add new events or plot twists—whatever you need to make your script interesting. When your script seems finished and polished enough, write a final draft and hand it in.

Remember to follow these script writing rules:

1. Write the title at the top. List the characters.

2. Number each scene and give it a title.

3. Describe the setting where the scene takes place.

4. Underline the characters' names. Start dialogue on the line below the name. Leave an extra line between characters.

5. Put stage directions in parentheses. Then the actors will know what you want them to do—without reading your stage directions out loud as part of the script.

Before you hand in your final draft, check your script for these common problems. Check any you find, then go back and fix them. If you need help, ask your teacher. Or see if your class can have an open reading, where everyone reads their scenes or skits and the audience makes comments and suggestions.

☐ PROBLEM: The action changes suddenly, with no logical connection to what has come before. Examples: The time shifts; a new character appears; new problems come up.

☐ PROBLEM: Words are left out.

☐ PROBLEM: Stage directions are not in parentheses.

☐ PROBLEM: The scene or skit is not dramatic or interesting. Maybe the main character's goal is not clear. Maybe the obstacles are not serious enough.

☐ PROBLEM: The ending is flat and uninteresting.

Drama Appreciation

Now that you've had experience writing a scene or a skit, you can watch and read other plays with new understanding and appreciation. Try it! After watching or reading a short play or skit, do one or more of these activities.

You're the Director

Think about the people or characters in the play or skit. What were they like? Did they remind you of anyone? Decide which of your friends, family members, or other people you know could act those parts. In other words, you're the director. Make sure to cast people who seem most like the characters. Give a reason for each casting decision. On a separate sheet of paper, create a casting sheet like the one shown here and fill it in with your casting decisions.

CASTING SHEET

Character in original play	Person I would cast in the part	My reason for casting that person
Jeff in the After-School Special	Jeremiah	He seems to know about the kinds of problems the character faces
Sarah in the skit we read in class	Amanda	She has the same attitude about school as Sarah

Character Critiques

Critique the characters in the play or skit. Who was the main character? Was there more than one main character? Which characters were there just to help the play or skit move along? Once you have the characters in mind, think about and answer these questions:

◆ Which characters had very little to do?

◆ Who were the main "bad guys"? (This includes both male and female characters.)

◆ Who were the main "good guys"? (Both male and female characters.)

◆ If you had to eliminate some characters without destroying the play or skit, which characters would you choose?

◆ Which character seemed the most believable or realistic?

◆ Which character seemed the least believable or realistic?

◆ If you were the playwright, what would you change about any or all of the characters?

Symbols

Symbols can add interest and depth to a play or skit. They communicate without dialogue or description. Everyone in the audience knows what they mean. For example, if a character is unshaven, dirty, and uses bad language, he might symbolize danger. If a character picks up a flag in a certain way, we can assume that he or she is patriotic. If a character wears unusual clothing or talks differently from everyone else in the play, we can expect him or her to be independent, with a unique outlook or perspective; perhaps that character will emerge as a leader.

Think of the play or skit you saw or read. Did you notice any symbols—any clues to indicate what a character was like, what the play was about, or something else the playwright wanted to communicate to you?

Different Roles

According to William Shakespeare, a famous playwright, "All the world's a stage, and all the men and women merely players...and one man in his time plays many parts." We are all actors; we all play many roles during our lifetime. You probably act differently at school than you do at home. You act differently at a party than you do on the job. You act differently to your sister or brother than you do to your friends or enemies.

List the roles you play. Do any of your roles remind you of the characters in the play or skit?

Publishing a Classroom Newsletter

n the next page, you'll find an example of a classroom newsletter. You might use it as a model for creating your first classroom newsletter.

English Composition

Northern Lights NewsLetter

October 19XX No. 4   Student Writing Project at North Middle School

Welcome Back Readers!

Introduction to the school year theme

By Sonny James—Lead Writer

Welcome to this year's first newsletter. The school theme this year is **"Strength Through Unity."** Let me tell you what this means to me.

To me, "Unity" means two things. First, I think it means we need to work together, help others, and respect each other. Second, I think it means cooperating with each other and agreeing to follow the school rules and listen to the teachers more.

When I think about "Strength," I see a school with fewer problems. This happens when we respect each other and also respect each others' property. I see strong teams and clubs and a sense of pride in what we can do together as a school.

For me personally, I'll try to tease people less. In this way, I'll show more respect for them. And if something goes wrong outside of school, I'll try not to bring those problems to school.

Miss Einsten says that our theme means many things to her. She told me that we have many people with different backgrounds and cultures at our school. We can be strong when we combine the strengths of all the different people in our school and work together for unity.

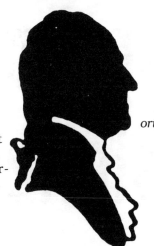

Like the 13 original colonies... We can have strength through unity

September Birthday Thoughts

Jesse Fillipa

Birthdays sneak up on you and they go by fast. This makes me sad because I don't like to get older. I'm not sure I want to be an adult—ever! (Too many responsibilities.) Two people I contacted during first period have September birthdays: (teacher) Karen Smithson and (student) Jason Lawrence. To all of the September birthdays in our class and school: Have a good one!

Strength Through Unity

By Shermie Edland
Lead Writer

North Middle School is the best
Better than all the rest.

We don't have to worry
We don't have to care
Because we know
In our hearts and minds
That our theme for this year
Will be there.

We can be the best
We can be strong
When "Strength Through Unity"
Is our song.

You'll start by working together as a class to select a theme for your newsletter. Some students will write articles on the theme, and others will use ideas from the Newsletter Planning Chart your teacher will give you. Lead stories are usually longer than other stories, require research, and go on the front page.

TIP: When you organize your article, use the "inverted pyramid." Put your most important ideas *first* rather than last. This is because articles are often shortened to fit the space available for them. Editors cut lines from articles starting at the end. If your important ideas come first, they won't be cut.

Make your best effort, since your newsletter will be read by others. Don't be afraid to ask for advice on how to organize your article. Many reporters talk with their editors ahead of time. If you are doing an interview, get help with writing the questions. Your editor or teacher will help you plan and then edit your first draft.

When you complete your final draft, your article will be entered into the computer for use later in a desktop publishing software program. If there is room, you will be able to choose a picture to go with your article. You might choose a picture from a clip art book, computer clip art disk, or art created by other students; you may decide to do your own illustration. The art must be in black-and-white. Use the computer to create headlines with computer graphics.

When your newsletter is complete, distribute it to students, teachers, school counselors, administrators, and other people you know. It will take about two to three weeks from start to finish to plan and publish your newsletter.

Imaginative Literature and Story Assignments

Characterization

fter you finish learning about a character in a story, movie, or book, there are many ways you can continue to enjoy the character. You might imagine the character at home. What television programs does he or she watch? Or you might imagine that you are having a conversation with the main character. What are some of the things you talk about? If the character wrote a will, what instructions would he or she include, and why? These are the kinds of questions you'll be asked to consider. To answer them, you'll have to stretch your imagination.

Wanted: Main Character

The main character in the story has just quit. It's your job to hire a replacement. Write a Help Wanted ad describing the kind of person you're looking for.

1. List six words or phrases that describe the main character. What was he or she really like? Fair, selfish, generous, kind, sensitive, strong, etc.? What did the main character look like? How did he or she act around others? (Examples: funny, shy, aggressive.)

    _____

    _____

    _____

    _____

    _____

    _____

2. Write a want ad for the "job" of main character in the story. What would you look for if you needed someone just like the character who quit? Keep your answers short.

    Wanted: Main Character. Need someone who is _____

    _____

    _____

    _____

    _____

The Report Card

If the main character attended your school, what subjects would he or she take? For example, would she take P.E. because she is athletic and likes to be outdoors? Would he take business courses because he likes to write letters? Would she sign up for Advanced Math because she's good with numbers? Would he take a child-care class because he enjoys helping people and likes to be around children? What kind of grades would the main character get?

Suppose the main character will take four required classes and two electives (classes of his or her choice). List the classes and the grades the main character might earn. Give your reasons in the form of "story clues"—insights into the character you gained from the story, movie, or book. Then grade the main character's work habits—again, using clues from the story, movie, or book.

Example:

Main character's name: _____

PERIOD	CLASS	GRADE
1	English (required) *Story clue:* She likes books and reading; she has a good vocabulary.	A
2	P.E. (required) *Story clue:* She doesn't like sports; she spends a lot of time indoors	C
3	History (required) *Story clue:* She seems to know a lot about the past	B+

Now complete your main character's report card.

Main Character's Name: _____

Required Courses and Electives

PERIOD	CLASS	GRADE
1	English (required) *Story clue:*	
2	Math (required) *Story clue:*	
3	Science (required) *Story clue:*	
4	P.E. (required) *Story clue:*	
5	_____ (elective) *Story clue:*	
6	_____ (elective) *Story clue:*	

Work Habits

PERIOD	CLASS	GRADE
1.	Follows directions.	
2.	Shows respect for other students.	
3.	Completes assignments on time.	
4.	Accepts criticism.	
5.	Comes to class prepared.	
6.	Is friendly and courteous.	
7.	Works hard in class.	

TV Guide

Pretend that you're the main character, and you're home for a week of vacation. You can watch any three TV programs you choose. What programs will you watch? Look through the TV schedule for the coming week, and list your three choices. Support your choices with story clues.

1. Program: _____

Story clues: _____

_____

2. Program: _____

Story clues: _____

_____

3. Program: _____

Story clues: _____

_____

Last Will and Testament

Your favorite character is about to fill out a Last Will and Testament. Think of possessions he or she treasures. Then decide who the character will leave these possessions to. (In other words, you must also think carefully about other characters in the story.)

If you can't think of any specific possessions owned by your favorite character, think of things he or she might like to own, based on story clues. Or think of things you own that the character might like to have.

```
┌─────────────────────────────────────────────────────────────┐
│                  LAST WILL AND TESTAMENT                      │
│  I, _____, being of sound mind and body, │
│  do hereby leave the following possessions to the persons named below: │
│  Possession                        Person                    │
│                                                              │
│  _____           _____  │
│                                                              │
│  _____           _____  │
│                                                              │
│  _____           _____  │
│                                                              │
│  Signature: _____        Date: _____         │
│  Witness: _____    │
└─────────────────────────────────────────────────────────────┘
```

The Great Escape

A hurricane is headed toward the place where the main character lives! He or she must leave immediately and can take only six special things. What will the character take? Why is each thing important to him or her? Remember to use story clues.

Warm up for this activity by thinking of what you would take and why if you were in this situation.

What I would take: Why it is important to me:

1. _____   _____

2. _____   _____

3. _____   _____

4. _____   _____

5. _____   _____

6. _____   _____

What the character would take: Why it is important to him or her:

1. _____   _____

2. _____   _____

3. _____   _____

4. _____   _____

5. _____   _____

6. _____   _____

The Counseling Session

Your favorite character is not very happy. After a whole week of feeling blue, the character decides to visit a counselor. The counselor reads 15 statements to the character. After reading each statement, the counselor asks, "Is this true for you?" Then they discuss some possible reasons why it is true. Afterward, the character feels much better.

Which of the following statements did the counselor check for his or her client (the character), and why? Give brief reasons, based on story clues.

CLIENT PROFILE

Client's name: _____ Date: _____

Prepared by Counselor: _____

CHECK IF TRUE	STATEMENTS	REASON(S)
___ 1.	I am very shy and find it hard to make friends.	_____
___ 2.	I'm stubborn and not very flexible.	_____
___ 3.	I'm not very attractive.	_____
___ 4.	I sometimes tell stories or exaggerate.	_____
___ 5.	I'm bored a lot. I can't think of anything to do.	_____
___ 6.	I take too many risks, like I'm trying to prove something.	_____
___ 7.	I worry a lot about my family or friends.	_____
___ 8.	I get angry a lot. I can't control my temper.	_____
___ 9.	I am not good at very many things.	_____
___ 10.	People at home don't understand me.	_____
___ 11.	I'm lonely a lot of the time.	_____
___ 12.	I can't tell when I'm really in love.	_____
___ 13.	I'm prejudiced or biased; I hate a lot of people.	_____
___ 14.	I don't know what I want to do with my life.	_____
___ 15.	I feel like I'm always under pressure.	_____

Extra Credit: Complete the profile for yourself and see how you compare with the character. Write about your similarities and differences.

Party Time

You've decided to have a dinner party for people in the story, movie, or book. You'll want to invite at least eight to ten people. If there are not enough characters in the story (or not enough you'd want to invite), complete the list with famous people you'd like to have as your guests. These might be famous living people or famous people from history—anyone you choose.

The people I will invite:

1. _____   6. _____
2. _____   7. _____
3. _____   8. _____
4. _____   9. _____
5. _____   10. _____

How will you seat your guests? You'll be dining at a long table. Some people might not get along. Some might prefer sitting next to others. Or you might come up with interesting combinations—a character beside a famous person.

On the table below, draw rectangles for place mats. Write the name of a guest in each place mat.

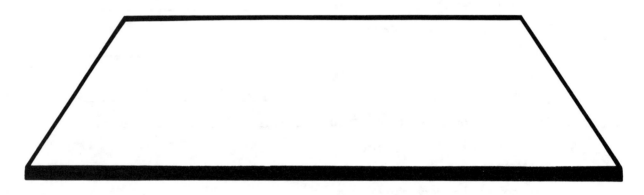

What will you serve at your dinner? Make up a menu. List the items in order of how they will be served.

1. _____
2. _____
3. _____
4. _____
5. _____
6. _____

Final Statement

The villain in the story has been sentenced to prison for life. Can you figure out what crime he or she might have committed? Fill out the Crime Report. (If the story doesn't have an obvious "villain," choose another character who seems likely to commit a crime.)

If the villain in the story really did commit a crime, you have a choice: report on that crime, using information from the story, or report on another crime the character could have committed, based on story clues.

CRIME REPORT

Perpetrator's name: _____

Date: _____

Description of the crime: _____

_____

_____

How the person was caught: _____

_____

_____

A reason (or reasons) why the person committed the crime: _____

_____

_____

Did the person seem sorry or remorseful? _____

_____

_____

What was the person's final request before going to prison? What did he or she want the public to know? _____

_____

_____

Doing Time

Bad news! The main character was just arrested for the crime of petty burglary. It's a very complicated story...hard to believe. The character claims that he or she was framed. The judge believes otherwise and sends the character to prison. After one year, the character applies for parole and lists you as a reference. The parole board invites you to the parole hearing, where they give you a copy of the character's Parole Observation Report. The other members of the parole board think the character should be set free, but the final decision rests with you. Complete the report, then decide whether the character should be paroled or remain in prison. Give your reasons—and remember to use story clues.

PAROLE OBSERVATION REPORT—CONFIDENTIAL

Subject's name: _____ Date: _____

Crime or crimes committed: _____

_____

_____

Duties or work performed in prison: _____

_____

_____

Condition of subject's cell (how has it been decorated? how has it been kept?):

_____

_____

Does the subject get along with other inmates? Explain: _____

_____

_____

Does the subject get along with the prison officials? Explain: _____

_____

_____

What does the subject spend most of his or her free time doing? _____

_____

_____

Do you believe the subject should be paroled? ☐ Yes ☐ No

State three reasons for your decision:

1. _____

2. _____

3. _____

The Dating Service

The main character is new in town and wants to meet people. So he or she goes to a dating service and fills out an application.

Imagine that you're the main character and complete the application. Use story clues.

• •

REMEMBER...

In this activity, you are writing as the main character. You are describing the character's appearance, interests, hobbies, etc. You are not describing yourself. Be sure to stay "in character" when you are answering the questions.

• •

"THE FRIENDSHIP CONNECTION" DATING SERVICE QUESTIONNAIRE—CONFIDENTIAL

Name: _____   Today's Date: _____
    (name of main character)

About you:

1. Describe your physical appearance.

    Height: _____ Weight: _____ Hair color: _____ Eye color: _____

2. Your health is (check one): ☐ Excellent ☐ Good ☐ Fair

    Do you work out or exercise regularly? ☐ Yes ☐ No

    If yes, describe what you do and how often: _____

    _____

    _____

3. Describe your interests.

    What kinds of movies do you like? _____

    _____

    List the titles of your two favorite movies: _____

    _____

What kinds of music do you like? _____

_____

List your two favorite albums, performers, or groups: _____

_____

What kinds of food do you like? _____

_____

List your two favorite restaurants: _____

_____

4. Describe what you do in your spare time.

    Your hobbies: _____

    _____

    Something you believe in strongly and would be willing to volunteer for:

    _____

    _____

    Other: _____

About the person you would like to meet:

5. What kind of person are you looking for? Describe his or her personality in
    two sentences: _____

    _____

    Describe his or her appearance: _____

    _____

6. What kind of job would you like your date to have? _____

    _____

7. Tell anything else about your date that is important to you:

    _____

8. Where do you plan to go on your first date together? _____

    _____

9. Describe your personality in two sentences. What kind of person are you?

    What are you like? _____

    _____

Setting and Plot

Like the activities about characterization, the ones in this section invite you to think more deeply about a story, movie, or book, using your imagination and story clues. Now you'll focus more closely on the setting and the plot.

The *setting* is the location (or locations) where most of the action takes place. Sometimes there are several settings and the action moves back and forth between places—and even between time periods. (Time is an important part of setting.) Characters often act differently in different settings. You'll practice describing, changing, imagining, and fantasizing about settings.

The *plot* is the story line that determines the sequence of events in the story. When you describe a plot, you tell what happens in a story, in order from beginning to end.

Warm up for this section by thinking about the following questions:

◆ *Did you like where the story happened? Would you have changed the setting?*

◆ *Did you like the way the story began? Would you have changed the beginning?*

◆ *Did you like the way the story ended? Would you have changed the ending?*

◆ *Would you have made the story shorter or longer?*

◆ *Could you have written a better story?*

The Travel Letter

Last summer, you had a unique travel opportunity. The publisher of the story paid your way to visit the setting. In return, you agreed to write a brief report about the setting. However, when you arrived at the setting, you noticed that you had lost your wallet—with all of your money, travelers' checks, and credit cards. Complete the following letter. Write as *yourself*—not as one of the story characters—but keep story clues in mind.

Today's Date: _____

Dear _____,

I have finally arrived in _____.
It's a great place. Already I've seen a few of the local sights, including

_____, _____,

and _____. I also met some interesting people

including _____ and _____.

When I think of home, what I miss the most is _____

_____.

I will be writing more about this place soon. At the moment, however, I have a big problem. I lost my wallet with all of my money, travelers' checks, and credit cards. Please send me $_____ right away!

Sincerely,

_____

P.S. _____

Travel Poster

Would you like to visit the setting where the story takes place? What is special about it? To answer these questions, you will design a travel poster that describes the setting.

Start by getting some travel posters or brochures from a travel agency. Study them carefully. What kinds of words and pictures do they use? How do they make you feel?

Answer the following questions about the story setting. Then use your answers and ideas to create your travel poster.

1. What three things about the setting do you remember most clearly? (Examples: the temperature, rain, sand, light, sounds, colors, buildings, excitement, mystery, darkness, etc.)

    _____

    _____

    _____

2. What colors come to mind when you think of the setting?

    _____

    _____

3. If you could visit the setting, what three sites or things would you most want to see?

    _____

    _____

    _____

4. What kinds of people would you be most likely to see?

    _____

    _____

    _____

5. What three things would you like to do there?

    _____

    _____

    _____

Give your travel poster a title. You might use the place name, the time, or a slogan that describes the setting. Examples: "Moscow," "California," "Mars," "The 12th Century," "Jolly Old England," "The Future," "The City of Lights," "Dinosaur Valley."

Your title: _____

Now create your poster. Include pictures cut from magazines, original drawings, slogans, colors, poems—anything you choose. You will want your poster to communicate your feelings about the story setting.

Pack Your Bags

You are going to visit the main character for five years. During that time, you will not be able to receive any packages from home. You will have to bring anything of yours that you think you will need—but you are limited to only ten items.

Think about the setting. What is the climate like? Will you be facing any special challenges or dangers? When does the story take place—in the present? the past? the future? Is there something you can't live without but you won't be able to get there? Is there anything you definitely *shouldn't* bring?

List the ten items you will bring along on your five-year visit. Give your reason(s) for choosing each one.

Item I need to bring: **My reason(s):**

1. _____   _____

2. _____   _____

3. _____   _____

4. _____   _____

5. _____   _____

6. _____   _____

7. _____   _____

8. _____   _____

9. _____   _____

10. _____   _____

You're the Cartoonist

Imagine that you're a cartoonist. (Maybe you really are.) It's your job to tell the entire plot of the story in a Sunday newspaper cartoon strip. Determine the six main events that happen in the story. Draw the cartoons (or write a description of what you would draw). Then, beneath each cartoon (or description), write a few words or a sentence about the event.

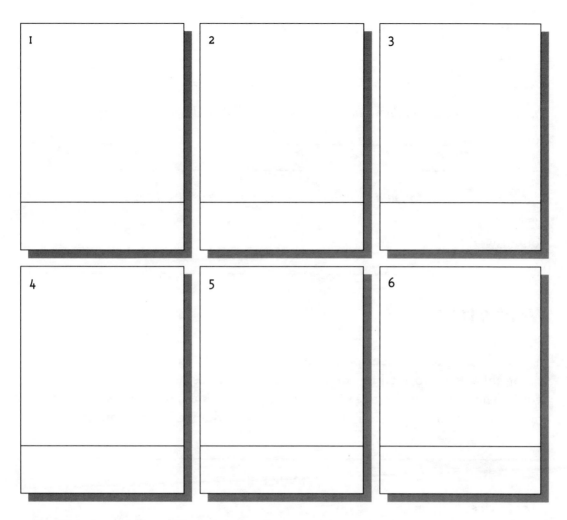

Predicting the Character's Future

The story is over, and the main character doesn't know what happens next...
but you do. The character comes to you for advice. Based on what you learned
about the character from the story, predict his or her future. (If the main character dies in the story, choose another character to write about.)

The character asks, "Where will I be living five years from now?"

You answer: " _____

_____."

The character asks, "Will I have a lot of money and/or a good job?"

You answer: " _____

_____."

The character asks, "Will I help others? How will this happen? What will I do?"

You answer: " _____

_____."

The character asks, "Will I be happy or sad? Tell me why."

You answer: " _____

_____."

The character asks, "Is there anyone or anything I should watch out for?"

You answer: " _____

_____."

The character asks, "Should I change anything about myself if I want to be more successful?"

You answer: " _____

_____."

What's It Worth?

The main character worked hard in the story, and he or she is now submitting an invoice (bill) for services performed. Complete the invoice. List the six most important acts performed by the character and decide how much each one is worth. The minimum fee is $10 per act. If you think a particular act took a long time to do or required a great deal of effort, the fee should reflect this.

INVOICE

For Services Performed

Name: _____

Social Security Number: _____

Act		Fee
I.	_____	_____
2.	_____	_____
3.	_____	_____
4.	_____	_____
5.	_____	_____
6.	_____	_____

TOTAL DUE: $ _____

Payment is due upon receipt of invoice.

You're the Editor

Most stories you read are edited before they are published. (Movie scripts also go through several editing and writing stages.) Pretend that the story or book you read was never edited. You have just read it in first draft form. What changes would you make to the story? What parts will you ask the author to rewrite? Complete the following letter as if you are writing to the author. (If you are writing about a movie, imagine that you have read the script.)

STUDENT OPINION PUBLISHING HOUSE

Dear _____,

I enjoyed reading your new story titled _____.
While we here at Student Opinion Publishing House feel that your story can be successful, we would like to suggest that you make some changes. Please look over my list of suggestions. We believe that they can help to make your story more interesting.

1. _____

2. _____

3. _____

4. _____

5. _____

6. _____

We will be happy to consider publishing or producing your story once you have completed the revisions outlined above. If you have any questions, don't hesitate to call.

Sincerely,

_____

Editor

Student Opinion Publishing House

PART 3

Exciting Reporting

Introduction

he assignments in Part 3 of *Exciting Writing, Successful Speaking* give you a chance to practice your skills on longer projects. You'll design and conduct a survey, prepare an easy book report, write a report about the story of your life (an autobiography), and write a report about something you are interested in (like a hobby). You will find these skills useful in the future when you're asked to write term papers or reports in English, science, or social studies class. Because these projects take time, you may work on them a little each day or each week.

Doing a Survey

Have you ever been asked to take part in a survey? Did you enjoy giving your opinion? (Most people do.) Did you know that survey results can affect your life? For example, if a survey showed that a large percent of the population thought the driving age should be lowered (or raised), it could happen. If most people believed that school should last year-round, summer vacation could be a thing of the past.

We often use survey results to determine what people think about a given issue. Then the results are used to predict how people might respond to a new policy (or a new movie, or a new product). In this way, a survey can be used to guide your plans for the future.

In this assignment, you'll learn the different steps that go into designing a survey questionnaire and preparing a report on your results.

Easy Book Reports

For a change of pace, try relaxing with a story from a book or magazine. Share with others what you read. Writing book reports is another skill that will come in handy in future classes (or classes you're taking right now).

Writing a Short Report: The (Auto)Biography

You'll get a chance to write the best story of your life—a story *about* your life (or the life of someone you know well). You'll collect facts and organize them in an interesting way.

Writing a Longer Report

You'll use the skills you practiced in writing your autobiography to prepare a report on a topic of special interest to you. Your report might be about skateboarding, sports, cooking, fashion, music, living on your own, getting a job— whatever you like. Or it might be about a social issue that concerns you, such as homelessness, the environment, animal abuse, drug abuse, and so on. Or it might be about your home town, the lives of special older citizens, or the future of space travel. The choice is yours.

Doing a Survey

ach day, hundreds—sometimes thousands—of people are asked to take part in surveys. Usually, surveys are done by private companies and government agencies that specialize in asking survey questions and interpreting survey information.

Companies, newspapers, state agencies, and the federal government all conduct surveys. (The United States Census is a type of survey.) School administrators or parent-teacher organizations might survey students and parents to learn their opinions about school policies. They might ask questions like "Do you think radios should be banned on campus?" or "Do you think our school should have a dress code?" Politicians use surveys to find out what the voters "back home" are thinking and feeling. They might ask questions like "Do you support the President's new tax program?" or "Do you think our country should get involved in a war overseas?"

Can you list up to five more types of organizations, groups, or people who might want to have surveys done?

Many people do survey work for a living. People who conduct surveys use a list of questions on a survey form. They use this form like a script to interview people face-to-face, over the telephone, or through the mail. As you're about to discover, there are several different ways to ask questions and collect information for a survey. Once you learn some of these ways, you'll write questions and statements for your own survey.

Survey Question Warm-Ups

Yes-or-No Questions

Should the speed limit be raised on interstate highways?

☐ *Yes*   ☐ *No*

This is a simple yes-or-no question. There are no possible answers besides "yes" and "no."

Write a yes-or-no question about lowering the driving age.

_____

_____

Fill-In Questions

How many hours do you spend in the shower per week? _____

How many times per month do you go to the store? _____

Fill-in questions usually ask "how many," "how often," or "when." They specify a particular time span—*per* week, day, month, year, etc. The answer often requires a number.

Write a fill-in question about school attendance.

_____

_____

Forced-Choice Questions

Which of the following is most important in being popular? Check one:

___ *a.   Having money*

___ *b.   Having a car*

___ *c.   Having a nice personality*

___ *d.   Having a sense of humor*

___ *e.   Dressing in the current styles*

Forced-choice questions ask people to choose from a limited number of possible answers. For example, if you asked everyone in your school, "What does it take to be popular?," they might say anything. If you asked 500 students, you could get 500 different answers. A forced-choice question like the one above limits the number of possible answers. These answers can be added up and looked at to learn something about popularity in your school. (Does it depend mostly on material things? Does it depend mostly on personality?)

Write a forced-choice question about current issues in your school.

_____

_____

___ a. _____

___ b. _____

___ c. _____

___ d. _____

___ e. _____

Scale-of-Agreement Questions

I think school should run all year, with vacations spread out across 12 months.

Strongly Agree		Unsure		Strongly Disagree
5	4	3	2	1

A scale-of-agreement question is really a statement, not a question. The purpose is to find out how strongly other people agree or disagree with the statement.

Write a scale-of-agreement statement about how much homework is assigned in your school.

_____

_____

Strongly Agree		Unsure		Strongly Disagree
5	4	3	2	1

Some scale-of-agreement statements use a scale of 1 to 10 or 1 to 3.

Designing Your Survey

Working with one or more partners, make up a survey questionnaire about a topic of interest to you. Follow these steps.

1. List the members of your survey team.

◆ _____

◆ _____

◆ _____

◆ _____

2. List 2-4 topics you might want to do a survey about.

    ◆ _____

    ◆ _____

    ◆ _____

    ◆ _____

    Together, choose one topic you would like to write survey questions about. Make sure this is a topic that won't embarrass your class or the people you'll be surveying. Otherwise you might not get answers to your questions.

    Write your topic here: _____

    IMPORTANT: Get your topic approved before going any further.

    Teacher's signature: _____

3. Jason and Sara developed a survey to find out if the students in their class would like to go to school year round, with vacations spread out across 12 months. Some of the things they wanted to find out about were:

◆ *Do students get bored toward the end of the summer?*

◆ *Would they enjoy having 1 month off every 4 months?*

◆ *How many students need to work full-time in the summer?*

◆ *How many students feel that they forget a lot over the summer?*

◆ *How many students feel that they would do better in school if they went to school year round?*

    Sara and Jason didn't just come out and ask the big question, "Do you want school to last all year?" Instead, they tried to "tease out" the other students' feelings, values, and opinions by asking indirect questions. These are also called *inferential* questions. They hint at the big question without asking it directly.

    List 5 issues or concerns related to your topic that you'd like to learn more about.

    ◆ _____

    ◆ _____

    ◆ _____

    ◆ _____

    ◆ _____

Now rewrite these issues or concerns as indirect (inferential) questions. These questions should help you to "tease out" or discover another person's feelings, values, and opinions without asking about them directly.

◆ _____
_____

◆ _____
_____

◆ _____
_____

◆ _____
_____

◆ _____
_____

4. It's important that your questions not be biased. In other words, if you have an opinion about the topic, your opinion shouldn't show through your questions.

    Following are 3 questions Jason and Sara wrote. Their teacher told them that 2 of their questions were biased and one was unbiased, or neutral. Can you identify which questions the teacher meant? Start by reading each question. For each, check "biased" or "neutral."

    ☐ Biased   *a.   Would you like to have the advantages of an all-year-round school?*
    ☐ Neutral

    ☐ Biased   *b.   Would you consider changing to an all-year-round school if you knew more about it?*
    ☐ Neutral

    ☐ Biased   *c.   Why would an all-year-round school be better than our current 9-month school year?*
    ☐ Neutral

Which questions make you feel that Sara and Jason want an all-year-round school? These are the biased questions. Which words reveal their bias? These are called "loaded" words. Underline the loaded words in the biased questions above.

Now rewrite the biased questions so they don't contain any loaded words.

◆ _____
_____

◆ _____
_____

Look over the questions you wrote in #3 above. Do you see any loaded words? Do any of your questions give away your opinion? Rewrite any biased questions to make them neutral. Eliminate loaded words.

◆ _____
_____

◆ _____
_____

◆ _____
_____

◆ _____
_____

◆ _____
_____

5. Select 4 of your questions and put them in the 4 different forms you learned in the Survey Warm-Ups activity.

    A. Yes-or-No Question

        An example from Jason and Sara's survey:

        Have you ever heard of an all-year-round school?

        ☐ *Yes* ☐ *No*

        Your yes-or-no question:

        _____
        _____

B. Fill-In Question

Remember to ask "how many," "how often," or "when" and to specify a time frame if needed.

An example from Jason and Sara's survey:

At what point in the summer do you begin thinking about the next school year? What week and what month would that usually be?

Your fill-in question:

_____

_____

C. Forced-Choice Question

An example from Sara and Jason's survey:

Which of the following reasons would make all-year-round school attractive to you?

___ *a. I get bored in the summer*

___ *b. I forget too much over the summer*

___ *c. I'd love to be able to take a vacation in the fall*

Your forced-choice question:

___ a. _____

___ b. _____

___ c. _____

___ d. _____

___ e. _____

D. Scale-of-Agreement Question (Statement)

Jason and Sara's example:

How much do you agree or disagree with the following statement? "I would like the school board to consider a all-year-round school for the future."

Strongly Agree		Unsure		Strongly Disagree
5	4	3	2	1

Your scale-of-agreement question:

_____

_____

Strongly Agree		Unsure		Strongly Disagree
5	4	3	2	1

E. Write one or more survey questions using any form you choose.

_____

_____

_____

_____

_____

6. Ask someone (like a teacher) to review your questions, using the following checklist. If all items are checked, go on to the next step. If some items are not checked, ask which questions may need to be changed. Rewrite the questions and ask the teacher to review them again.

☐   The questions make sense and seem to fit the same topic.

☐   The questions are different—they don't repeat themselves.

☐   The questions are neutral, without loaded or biased words.

☐   The questions won't embarrass anyone. They are not too personal or direct.

7. Look over your questions and try to predict how people will answer them. In science, this is called developing a hypothesis. After you get answers to your survey, you'll be able to evaluate your hypothesis. How accurate was it? How close did you come to predicting what people would say? Assume that you ask 20 people your questions. How do you think most people will answer? Write your predictions.

◆   _____

_____

◆   _____

_____

◆   _____

_____

◆ _____

_____

_____

◆ _____

_____

_____

8. Design a survey form that you and your partner(s) can use with several different people. It might take a number of drafts before you get it just the way you want it. To help you think about your final survey form, look over Sara and Jason's survey on pages 154–155. Then answer the questions on page 156.

Notice that Sara and Jason's form includes space for the name of the survey taker (in this case, either Sara or Jason) and the date the survey was done (if the survey takes place over several days, the dates written in should show this). It also includes a brief statement about where Sara and Jason are from and why they are doing the survey. Each letter under a question—a through i—indicates one person being surveyed.

When you do a survey, you should always start by getting the other person's permission to ask the questions. You might say something like "Would you mind answering a few questions for my survey? It should only take about five minutes." If the person agrees, identify yourself and state the topic of your survey. Afterward, thank the person for his or her time.

SARA AND JASON'S SURVEY

Name of survey taker: <u>Sara deLong</u>

Date: <u>October 15, 1993</u>

Where we are from and the purpose of our survey:

<u>Mr. Howard's class at Barton School</u>

<u>Topic: Should we have an all-year-round school?</u>

THE SURVEY QUESTIONS

1. Yes-or-No Question

    Have you ever heard of an all-year-round school?

    a. ☐ Yes ☐ No   d. ☐ Yes ☐ No   g. ☐ Yes ☐ No

    b. ☐ Yes ☐ No   e. ☐ Yes ☐ No   h. ☐ Yes ☐ No

    c. ☐ Yes ☐ No   f. ☐ Yes ☐ No   i. ☐ Yes ☐ No

2. Fill-In Question

    At what point during the summer do you look forward to returning to school?
    After how many months of vacation?

    a. ___   d. ___   g. ___

    b. ___   e. ___   h. ___

    c. ___   f. ___   i. ___

3. Forced-Choice Question

    Which of the following reasons would make all-year-round school attractive to you?

    (i) I get bored in the summer.

    a. ___   d. ___   g. ___

    b. ___   e. ___   h. ___

    c. ___   f. ___   i. ___

    (ii) I forget too much over the summer.

    a. ___   d. ___   g. ___

    b. ___   e. ___   h. ___

    c. ___   f. ___   i. ___

(iii) I'd love to have a vacation in the fall.

a. ___   d. ___   g. ___

b. ___   e. ___   h. ___

c. ___   f. ___   i. ___

(iv) School is too long. I'm too tired by the time summer vacation comes.

a. ___   d. ___   g. ___

b. ___   e. ___   h. ___

c. ___   f. ___   i. ___

4. Scale-of-Agreement Question

How much do you agree or disagree with the following statement? "I would like the school board to consider an all-year-round school for the future."

Strongly Agree		Unsure		Strongly Disagree
5	4	3	2	1
a	a	a	a	a
b	b	b	b	b
c	c	c	c	c
d	d	d	d	d
e	e	e	e	e
f	f	f	f	f
g	g	g	g	g
h	h	h	h	h
i	i	i	i	i

Questions about Sara and Jason's Survey:

◆ Is there a way to quickly record each person's answers on the survey form? ☐ Yes ☐ No

◆ How many people can be surveyed with this form? _____

(You'll want your survey form to have answer spaces for up to 10 people. Or make one copy of your form for each person you plan to survey.)

◆ What one question on the survey would you change?

    ☐ the yes-or-no question

    ☐ the fill-in question

    ☐ the forced-choice question

    ☐ the scale-of-agreement question

◆ Do you agree with the following statement?

"I could make my survey form look just like Sara and Jason's."

Strongly Agree		Unsure		Strongly Disagree
5	4	3	2	1

9. When you're finished with your survey form, type it or neatly print it and get it approved.

Teacher's signature: _____

10. Divide the following tasks among the members of your group. Decide who will do what to get the survey done.

TASK	WHO DOES IT? (Everyone or a certain person?)	WHEN IT MUST BE DONE BY (Date)
Prepare your final survey form. Make one copy for each member of your group.		
Survey 10 people each. (Do more if you have time.)		
Add up the responses for each question. Compute percentages.		
Make a chart or spreadsheet to show the responses.		
Write a written report. (The directions are given in the next section.)		
Give an oral report to the class, using the written report as your guide.		

Writing a Survey Report

Writing a survey report is easier than it sounds. Start by adding up the responses for each question. Then turn these totals into averages or percentages, or list your results on a line or continuum in terms of "from most to least." You can also chart your results, or use a spreadsheet-charting program that does this automatically. Finally, write a description of your survey results. It might help to study Jason and Sara's report before you begin. Feel free to borrow some of their words and ideas if they will help you to prepare your report. Use the Survey Report Form you teacher will give you or create your own.

JASON AND SARA'S SURVEY REPORT

I. THE PURPOSE OF OUR SURVEY

    A.   State your topic and why you chose it. Write your original prediction or hypothesis.

        We chose the topic "All-Year-Round School." We like the idea and wondered if other people felt the same way about it. Our original hypothesis was "Most people would like the all-year-round schedule better than the one we have now, with 9 months of school and a 3 month summer vacation."

    B.   Describe your general or main question.

        We were basically asking people the following general or main question in our survey: "Would you consider changing to an all-year-round school if you knew more about it?"

II. THE METHOD WE USED FOR OUR SURVEY

    A.   Describe who did what.

        We discussed the survey questions, and Jason wrote them down. Then the teacher gave us some ideas for improving our questions. Sara re-typed the questions onto a form we could use.

    B.   Tell where the survey was done and who was surveyed.

        We conducted our survey at lunch. We asked 30 people in the milk ticket line.

    C.   Describe how people reacted when you asked them to take part in your survey. Did they enjoy the survey?

        People seemed to enjoy being asked their opinions about an all-year-round school.

    D.   Tell how many people you surveyed. (In some surveys, this is called the "N".) Then tell if you think your sample was large enough to represent most people's views.

        We planned to survey a total of 40 people, but we collected data from only 30 people. We feel that this is a large enough sample to give us good results.

III. TOTALS AND RESULTS

Write down each question. Figure the totals, averages, or percentages for each response. (Get help from your teacher if you need it to complete this step.)

We asked the four questions below. The results are shown after each question.

1. *Have you ever heard of an all-year-round school?* _____

    YES: 21 (70%)

    NO: 6 (20%)

    NO ANSWER: 3 (10%)

2. *At what point during the summer do you look forward to returning to school? After how many months of vacation?*

    3 MONTHS: 9 people (30%)

    2 MONTHS: 15 people (50%)

    1 MONTH: 3 people (10%)

    NEVER: 3 people (10%)

    The average time seemed to be about 2 months.

3. *Which of the following reasons would make all-year-round school attractive to you?*

    I GET BORED IN THE SUMMER: 6 people (20%)

    I FORGET TOO MUCH OVER THE SUMMER: 6 people (20%)

    I'D LOVE TO HAVE A VACATION IN THE FALL: 15 people (50%)

    SCHOOL IS TOO LONG: 3 people (10%)

    Most people would like to have a vacation in the fall.

4. *How much do you agree or disagree with the following statement? "I would like the school board to consider an all-year-round school for the future."*

    STRONGLY AGREE: 15 (50%)

    UNSURE: 6 (20%)

    STRONGLY DISAGREE: 9 (30%)

    NOTE: We grouped the 1 and 2 scores and the 4 and 5 scores together.

    ◆   *15 (50%) seemed to agree and scored 4 or higher.*

    ◆   *6 (20%) scored a 3 or unsure.*

    ◆   *9 (30%) disagreed and scored a 2 or lower.*

IV. CONCLUSION AND RECOMMENDATIONS

A. Tell which survey result(s) supported your original hypothesis.

The results for questions 1 and 3 came closest to what we predicted. We thought that most people would have heard about an all-year-round school. Also, we thought that most people would like to have a vacation in the fall.

B. What surprised you about your survey totals? Which responses did you not predict very well?

We were surprised that most people start thinking about school after only 2 months of vacation. We thought it would be longer.

C. Can you make any recommendations based on your survey results? What does your survey seem to prove or suggest?

We think our survey shows that people are interested in considering an all-year-round school. For example, most people (about 90%) start looking forward to school before summer is over. Maybe summer is too long. Also, 50% of the people we surveyed would like the school board to consider an all-year-round school for the future, and 20% were unsure, which means that only 30% thought the board should NOT consider an all-year-round school.

Therefore, based on our survey, we recommend that the school board consider the idea of having an all-year-round school.

Easy Book Reports and the Reading Journal

Starting Your Reading Journal

Book reports are required in most English classes. This lesson illustrates an easy way to write an outline for a book report. You can also use this outline to prepare an oral book report.

Start by selecting a book you want to read. It should be a work of fiction (a story with characters rather than a how-to book or other work of nonfiction). It should be at least 75 to 100 pages long, or you might choose to read two 50-page books. You must read the book by the deadline given. To help you meet the deadline, bring the book to school every day, because you will often find moments both in and outside of class when you can do some reading.

To help you keep track of your story and the characters, you'll write about what you read in a reading journal. Your teacher will give you a form to use, or you might design your own form or write your journal in a spiral-bound notebook. You will turn in your journal every so often to be checked by your teacher. You'll use ideas from your reading journal in your written and oral book reports.

Writing a Short Book Report

When you are finished reading your book, use the notes you wrote in your reading journal to write an outline report about the book. Follow the sample shown below. Use Roman numerals for your main headings, and be sure to indent the letters A, B, and C. Save your outline in case you are asked to give an oral book report; it will work very well for your speech outline.

SAMPLE BOOK REPORT OUTLINE

I.   TITLE: *The Silent Worm*

II. AUTHOR: *Mark Kay*

III. MAIN CHARACTERS: Write each character's name and a brief description.

   A. *Joseph was the father. He was mean.*

   B. *Helen was the mother. She had two jobs.*

   C. *Tony was their son. He wanted to run away.*

   D. *Ellen was the sister. She teased Tony a lot.*

IV. PLOT: List 6 to 10 main events in the story that together describe what happened. A main event is a time in the story when something important started or ended or a character changed. Begin each sentence with words like "first, second, then, next, finally."

   A. *First, Tony has a fight with his sister.*

   B. *Second, Joseph yells at Tony. They have a lot of arguments.*

   C. *Third, Tony decides to leave home.*

   D. *Next, his mother finds out.*

   E. *Then Tony learns that his mother is unhappy too. They both discuss leaving.*

   F. *Next, Tony and his mother find out that Joseph, the father, has a brain tumor. This makes the dad act terrible. He is not himself.*

   G. *Finally, the dad goes for an operation and gets better.*

V. SAMPLE PASSAGE: Copy a few lines that show the author's writing style. Look for parts that you like best and choose one or two.

VI. WOULD YOU RECOMMEND THIS BOOK?

    A. Describe what you liked best about the book. Tell why you liked it.

    I liked the main characters. They seemed real. The mother was nice.

    B. Choose a sample passage to read out loud. You will read it as part of your oral book report.

    Sample passage: bottom of page 3 to top of page 5.

    C. Describe what you liked least about the book. Tell why you didn't like it.

    I didn't like the beginning. It started out too slow. I also didn't like the father or sister at first.

    D. Would you recommend this book? Who do you think should read it? Tell why.

    Yes, I would recommend that other students read this book. I think they'll enjoy the main characters. It also has a valuable message for the reader.

Giving an Oral Book Report

Start by making some short notes for your report, or use your book report outline (if you wrote one). Practice your speech with your notes or outline. TIP: As you practice, use your finger to keep your place on your outline. This way, you can get in the habit of looking up every so often to establish eye contact. When you look down again, your finger will show you where to resume your speech.

You will be rated on your performance. Your teacher will give everyone a copy of the Speaker Rating Form for Oral Book Report, but you will be rated by only three people: you, your teacher, and another student of your choice. Study the form so you know what you will be rated on and how to use the form when you are asked to rate someone else. If you are not sure what you are supposed to do, ask for help or a demonstration.

Before giving your oral book report, you may want to review the lesson on Public Speaking in Part 2 of *Exciting Writing, Successful Speaking*. See if your teacher will let you practice some of the voice and gesture games if you need a refresher course.

Writing a Short Report: The (Auto)Biography

You will soon be writing about one of the most interesting things you know: your life.* You will be writing an *autobiography,* your own life story. It may take a few pages, but your life is worth it! Along the way, you'll learn and practice the skills of outlining, note-taking, and preparing a bibliography. You'll use many of the paragraph-organizing skills you learned in earlier assignments. After you finish writing your autobiography, you may be asked to give an oral report or speech about it.

_____

If you have already done this assignment, or if you don't want to write about your life, you may write a *biography* (someone else's life story) instead. Choose someone you know very well.

You'll research your topic by asking questions about your life and yourself. What has made you the way you are? What people have been important in your life? What events or experiences have shaped your thoughts? What do you think is important in life? What do you hope the future will bring? The Life Questionnaire on pages 165–172 will help you to gather your thoughts and facts. You may not be able to use all of the information from all of the questions, but you'll find that answering each question gives you another way to look at yourself. You will have to decide which information to include in your autobiography.

Report Writing Steps

When preparing a report, there are several steps all writers go through. First, you choose a topic; in this case, the topic is you. Next, you collect information about your topic. This is called *researching* your topic, and writers often put the information they collect on note cards. You'll learn more about note cards in the final project in *Exciting Writing, Successful Speaking*; for now, you'll collect your information on a questionnaire. You may find that the best way to answer some of the questions is by getting advice from or talking to someone who knows you well. After gathering your information, you must organize it. Putting your main ideas into an outline is the simplest way to organize your information.

When you have outlined your ideas, you'll be ready to start writing your first draft. As in 4-Step Writing, be sure to write on every other line to leave space for revisions and new ideas. After your rough draft is done, it's time to revise and edit. You'll type your final draft or write it in ink—but before you do that step, you'll need to list all of your sources of information, or *references*. A list of your references is called a *bibliography*, and it is usually the last page of a report or paper.

Before handing in your final draft, consider creating a cover; make a good impression! Your report may be one your teacher keeps to show to other students. It may be sent to the library so other students can use it as a reference in their reports. Future students might check out your report, just like a book or a magazine. They might even quote your words. Naturally, you'll have to turn in your report *on time*—by the final due date.

Look back over the description of report writing—the three paragraphs you just finished reading. Can you find the nine main steps in report writing? Look for these signal words:

after	before	for now
at last	first	next

Write these steps on the Steps and Schedule form your teacher will give you:

1. Choose a topic
2. Collect information
3. Organize information into an outline
4. Write the first draft
5. Revise and edit first draft
6. Prepare a bibliography
7. Write the final draft (typed or in ink)
8. Make a cover
9. Turn in the final draft on the due date

To finish your report on time, you'll need to plan ahead. Once you know your final deadline (due date), work backwards. Think about how much time you'll need to complete each step. Add the dates to the Steps and Schedule page. Fill in a Steps and Schedule page whenever you start a short report; it will help you to keep track of what you need to do and when you need to do it.

Life Questionnaire

IMPORTANT

Before you start writing, read the entire questionnaire, from beginning to end, and think about the questions. Then brainstorm the references or sources you will use to find answers. A reference or source can be anyone or anything— a person, club or agency, book, video, magazine, telephone call to an expert, etc.—that provides you with information or advice for your report. Because you are writing about yourself, you may use some unusual references or sources, like phone calls to relatives, family photo albums, baby books, family trees, and birth certificates. All of your references and sources will be listed in the bibliography at the end of your report.

Brainstorming References and Sources

You will need to use at least three references or sources for your report. After reading the questionnaire, think about three people you could ask for information or advice about your topic. (You may include yourself as one of your references or sources.) List your references or sources here:

_____

_____

_____

The Questions

The name of the person you are researching: _____

Your Family

1. Describe your family. Who are the adults you live with? (Examples: one or both parents, step-parents, guardians, foster parents, other relatives, etc.):

    _____

    _____

    How many brothers and sisters do you have? _____

    Who else is in your household? _____

    Do you have any pets? If so, describe them: _____

    _____

2. Tell about the work your parents (or other adults in your household) do:

    _____

    _____

    Do they like their work? _____

    _____

3. List your three favorite relatives (parents, aunts, uncles, grandparents, cousins, etc.):

    a. _____

    b. _____

    c. _____

4. Of all the people you are related to or live with, who are you *most* like and why? _____

    _____

Places You Have Lived

5. How many times has your family moved? _____

    Write about three to five places you have lived and the approximate dates.

    a.

    From when to when   Place

    _____   _____

    _____   _____

What I remember most about this place (or what I liked best about it):

_____

_____

b.
From when to when   Place

_____   _____

_____   _____

What I remember most about this place (or what I liked best about it):

_____

_____

c.
From when to when   Place

_____   _____

_____   _____

What I remember most about this place (or what I liked best about it):

_____

_____

d.
From when to when   Place

_____   _____

_____   _____

What I remember most about this place (or what I liked best about it):

_____

_____

e.
From when to when   Place

_____   _____

_____   _____

What I remember most about this place (or what I liked best about it):

_____

_____

Moments in Your Life

6. The funniest thing that ever happened to me: _____

   _____

   _____

7. The most embarrassing thing that ever happened to me: _____

   _____

   _____

8. The strangest thing that ever happened to me: _____

   _____

   _____

9. The most serious illness in my life: _____

   _____

   _____

10. Write about the most important thing that happened to you for every five years in your life. (Example: "Ages 1-5: My little sister was born when I was four. Suddenly I wasn't the only child anymore! It made a BIG difference.")

    Ages 1-5: _____

    _____

    Ages 6-10: _____

    _____

    Ages 11-15: _____

    _____

    Ages 16-21: _____

    _____

11. Write about your most important interests or activities for every five years in your life. (Example: "Ages 6-10: I discovered painting. I started painting pictures and sometimes painted on the walls of our apartment!")

    Ages 1-5: _____

    _____

    Ages 6-10: _____

    _____

    Ages 11-15: _____

    _____

Ages 16-21: _____

_____

Your Friends and Influences

12. Who is your best friend? _____

    Why do you like this person so much? _____

    _____

    What kinds of things do you do together? _____

    _____

13. Name the three *famous* people you most admire. Tell why you admire each person.

    a. _____

    _____

    b. _____

    _____

    c. _____

    _____

14. Name the three people you most admire who are *not famous* (but are important to you). Tell why you admire each person.

    a. _____

    _____

    b. _____

    _____

    c. _____

    _____

15. Name the three people who have most influenced your life. These might be friends, relatives, parents, teachers, coaches, employers, ministers, rabbis, other spiritual leaders, neighbors, etc. Tell how each person influenced you. (Example: "My father has been very important to me throughout my life. He always showed me how to use tools. I remember when he showed me how to carve wood and make furniture.")

    a. _____

    _____

    b. _____

    _____

c. _____

_____

Your Interests and Contributions

16. What kinds of movies do you like best?

_____AND

_____

17. What are your favorite subjects in school?

_____AND

_____

18. What kinds of music do you like best?

_____AND

_____

19. How do you help out around your home?

_____AND

_____

Other ways you help: _____

_____

20. Describe three times when you helped someone else. These might be times when you helped a friend in trouble, when you taught someone how to do something, or when you helped a relative, classmate, or neighbor.

a. _____

_____

_____

b. _____

_____

_____

c. _____

_____

_____

21. How do you want to be treated by others? _____

_____

_____

22. List three things you are good at doing. These might be things you enjoy doing in your spare time. Or they might be things you do so well that others often ask you to do them. They might be hobbies, games you enjoy, sports, musical instruments, volunteer activities—anything you choose to write about.

    a. _____

    _____

    b. _____

    _____

    c. _____

    _____

Big Questions

23. What is your most important value or personal belief? (Examples: truth, justice, honesty, fairness, trust, love, religious beliefs, open-mindedness, etc.) Why is it important to you? _____

    _____

24. What is your most important personal goal at this point in your life? _____

    _____

25. What is something you would like to do or become in the future? _____

    _____

26. How do you hope your life will change in the future? _____

    _____

27. What is one thing about you or your life that you would change right now, if you could? _____

    _____

28. What is one thing about you or your life that you hope will always stay the same? _____

    _____

Thinking Back, Looking Ahead, Summing Up

29. As you think back over your life, what has surprised you? Places? People? Events? Things? Do you begin to see that some people in your life have been more important than you first thought? Do you realize why you are good at certain things? Are you surprised at how your life has turned out so far? _____

_____

_____

_____

30. To summarize, list the ten most important things in your life so far. These might be people, places, experiences, surprises, beliefs, values, goals, hopes for the future—anything you would put in your personal Top Ten. They do not have to be in any particular order. Just list them.

_____

_____

_____

_____

_____

_____

_____

_____

_____

_____

Organizing and Outlining

Before you start writing, it's essential to organize your information, thoughts, and ideas. This keeps you from getting lost or stuck and makes sure that you say what you want and need to say.

An outline is an excellent way to get organized. An outline is built like a pyramid. At the peak is the theme, or Super Topic. The theme is like a title; it tells the whole story in a few words. Under the theme are the main topics. Each main topic will start a new paragraph. Finally, under each main topic are the subtopics, or details. These guide the writing of the paragraphs.

Following is an outline for an autobiography written by a student named Jennifer. She felt that her life was tough because her family was always moving, and she was always struggling to fit in and make new friends. She decided to write about this struggle and the ways she learned to cope. Notice that her theme included the word "struggle." Her three main topics were about people who taught her how to win, places where she learned valuable lessons, and ways in which she changed. After looking at Jennifer's outline, can you tell what her autobiography might have sounded like?

Theme	My Story: Learning from My Struggles
First Main Topic	I. The people who taught me how to compete to win
Subtopics	A. Uncle Jones, who taught me about sports
	B. Aunt Lucille, who taught me to work hard in school
	C. Teachers who encouraged me to try hard in math
Second Main Topic	II. Places where I had to learn to get along and prove myself
Subtopics	A. Winston, Illinois, where I played sports
	B. Carson City, Nevada—in body building club and winning a trophy
	C. Boise, Idaho—learning to fit into a new school
Third Main Topic	III. How I Changed
Subtopics	A. Stopped fighting so much
	B. Channeled my energies in school fund raisers
	C. Became more confident through sports
	D. Found teachers who liked me

TIP: Notice that each time Jennifer moved from a main topic to subtopics, she indented. So should you.

Organizing and Outlining Warm-Ups

With a little practice, you'll find that organizing and outlining become easy to do. Start by organizing each of the following lists into a logical order. Each should have one theme followed by three main topics. The rest of the items on the lists are details that fit into the subtopic level.

John's Report

John is writing a report about weekend entertainment. His ideas are listed below. How will you fit them into an outline? Some are already filled in to get you started. It's like putting together the pieces of a puzzle.

JOHN'S LIST

Weekend Entertainment

rent videos

check the library for free videos

play or watch sports

develop a hobby in a club

see films or movies

join a club for computer games

go to the movies

join a school team

find out about city sports leagues

go to watch a school game

join a club like model railroads

clubs for remote controlled cars

JOHN'S OUTLINE

Theme: Weekend Entertainment

First Main Topic

Subtopics

I.   *see films or movies*

   A.   *rent videos*

   B.   _____

   C.   _____

Second Main Topic

Subtopics

II.   *play or watch sports*

   A.   _____

   B.   _____

   C.   _____

Third Main Topic

Subtopics

III. _____

    A. _____

    B. _____

    C. _____

Susan's Report

Susan is writing a report about pets. Read her list, then complete her outline.

SUSAN'S LIST

common pets	*turtles*
There are many kinds of pets	*insect pets*
reptile pets	*dogs*
trained fleas	*ants*
snakes	*cats*
birds	*spiders*
frogs	

SUSAN'S OUTLINE

Theme _____

First Main Topic

Subtopics

I. _____

    A. _____

    B. _____

    C. _____

Second Main Topic

Subtopics

II. _____

    A. _____

    B. _____

    C. _____

Third Main Topic

Subtopics

III. _____

    A. _____

    B. _____

    C. _____

Writing Your Outline

Now it's time to take your ideas and organize them into an outline. Remember, an outline has main topics (shown by Roman numerals) followed by subtopics (shown by capital letters and indented).

Start by examining your ideas in your completed Life Questionnaire. Pay particular attention to your final list of the ten most important things in your life so far. Next, list all of the ideas you want to include in your autobiography. Then organize your list into an outline, just as you organized John's and Susan's lists in the warm-up activity. Your outline will guide you in writing your autobiography.

If you like, you may use the Outline Starter shown below to organize your list. Or create an original outline.

Using the Outline Starter

An outline starter is a set of directions for writing an outline. They are written in outline form. Simply follow this form and the directions to create your outline. You will need to add the names of people and places and other details to turn this starter into an outline you can use to write your autobiography. If you would rather create an original outline, skip ahead to the next section.

I.   The most important people and places in my life

    A. Tell about places you lived and what you liked about them

    B. Describe people you met in these places

    C. Tell how a person changed your life

II. How I have changed as I got older

    A. How you have changed at school

    B. How you have changed at home

    C. Changes you hope to make in the future

III. What I do and what I am interested in

    A. Tell about things you do well or are interested in

    B. Tell how you learned to do these things

    C. Tell about a how you might use these abilities at home, work, or school

    D. How you plan to get even better at these things

IV. My hopes and dreams

    A. Tell how you want to live after you leave school

    B. If you want a family, describe what you hope your family will be like

    C. Describe your ideal job

    D. If you have a dream about being famous, describe your dream

TIP: You can also use your outline for giving an oral report or a speech.

Creating an Original Outline

Start by deciding on your main topics. Following is a list of ideas that could be used for main topics. Which four or five would you like to write about?

- Important places in my life
- When I was a child
- Important moments in my life
- Important people in my life
- Ways in which I help others
- What I'm good at or like to do
- My dreams
- What I want from others
- How I have changed
- What I want to do when I get older
- What has stayed the same in my life
- What I enjoy doing most

Think of main topic headings for the four or five ideas you choose. Think of subtopics to list under your main topic headings. Write your main topic headings and subtopics on the Original Outline form your teacher will give you. Write your subtopics as short sentences or descriptive phrases. For now, don't worry about the Introduction and Conclusion.

Writing Your Introduction and Conclusion

Many writers know the trick of waiting until the end to write the introduction and conclusion. If you try to write them first, you may find it hard to get started. However, you may find that it is easier to write them—or at least jot down some ideas—once you know your main outline topics. Read over the examples shown next, then complete your own outline notes for an introduction and conclusion.

Following are some tips for writing introductory and concluding paragraphs, along with examples. When you start writing your first draft, come back to this page and look at the examples again. You may want to borrow from them. Just change a few key words.

Tips for Introductions

◆ Write your main topic.

I. *My Life Story*

◆ Write a simple introductory statement or question.

My report is an autobiography.

◆ List your subtopics and write a statement that summarizes your subtopics.

    A. the people in my life

    B. the places I have lived

    C. my hobbies and dreams

This report covers important people and places in my life. I will also discuss what I enjoy doing most and my dreams. For example....

◆ Include an opinion or observation.

I think my life has been very satisfying.

◆ OPTIONAL: Ask a question you hope to answer in your report.

One question I hope to answer is "What has made me what I am today?"

Tips for Conclusions

◆ State your conclusion in one line. Use a concluding phrase or word and repeat one of your most important ideas.

X. *In Conclusion...*

In conclusion, as I look back on my life, I think my family and friends have influenced me the most.

◆ List your subtopics and repeat any important ideas you especially want your reader to remember.

    A. my mom's values

    B. Uncle Willy's help

    C. coming to this school

My mother taught me my basic values. Uncle Willy helped me through school by helping with homework. Going to this school gave me a new chance to start over.

◆ Ask the reader a question to make him or her think. Or state your opinion. Or do both.

My coach once asked me, "Are you willing to sacrifice and achieve by working harder than the rest?" I'm still working on an answer. How would you answer this question? In my opinion, it is a question we can all ask ourselves.

Expanding Your Outline into a Final Report

Now it's time to turn your outline into a first (rough) draft. Remember to write on every other line. When you have finished this step, you'll begin the process of revising and editing your first draft. The last steps include creating a final draft, bibliography, and cover for your report.

Step 1: Expanding Your Outline

You'll begin by turning each subtopic in your outline into a complete thought. Think of this as a photographic process. You'll blow up, or enlarge, your negative (outline) into a photograph (report). Take each subtopic and add more details and examples. Here is an example of how Jennifer took her first main topic and subtopics and expanded them into a paragraph.

First Main Topic

Subtopics

I.   The people who taught me how to compete to win

    A.   Uncle Jones, who taught me about sports

    B.   Aunt Lucille, who taught me to work hard in school

    C.   Teachers who encouraged me to try hard in math

I learned the importance of trying hard and competing to win. I learned this from my relatives and teachers. My Uncle Jones was a good athlete and later a coach. He taught me several sports like soccer, basketball, and horse racing. He taught me the value of following a well-planned and disciplined training program. I was finally rewarded with a varsity letter. I also learned from my Aunt Lucille how to compete for grades. She would help me with homework. She taught me that competing at school is like winning a horse race. My teachers also encouraged me to try hard. I believe that I learned from all these people how to perform at my best. I had lots of people cheering me on to win, win, win!

Can you find the new ideas Jennifer added to her outline? Write two of them here: _____

_____

_____

_____

_____

Step 2: Writing the First (Rough) Draft

Remember to write in pencil and skip lines. If you can write your first draft on a word processor, it will be easy to make changes later.

When you finish your first draft, go back and make any changes or corrections. Turn in your first draft.

Step 3: Preparing the Final Draft

Make a good impression by typing your final draft or printing it out on a word processor. If you don't have access to a typewriter or word processor, write your final draft neatly in ink.

Step 4: Preparing the Bibliography

You'll learn more about bibliographies in the next project in *Exciting Writing*. For now, here's a basic introduction.

Make a list of the people you spoke to, the items you read, or the things you looked at or studied when gathering information for your autobiography. You need to be able to list at least three sources, and you may include yourself as a source. Follow this format when preparing your bibliography.

Resource (person, title, item, etc.)	Date (of conversation, publication, etc.)
_____	_____
_____	_____
_____	_____

Put your list in alphabetical order on a separate page. At the top of the page, write the word "Bibliography." This will be the last page of your report.

Step 5: Making a Cover

At last you're ready to put the frosting on the cake. In this final step, you'll create a cover for your report. Begin by thinking of a title; two to five words should be long enough (the best titles are short and catchy). Print your title in large, bold letters (use a computer if you can).

Your cover must also include three additional pieces of information besides the title:

◆ The name of the author (you)

◆ The date written (or due date)

◆ The class your report has been prepared for.

For ideas, study the samples.

Henry Williams *A man who never gives up* *By Eileen Sholski* Submitted 6-6-94 For Health Class	**JEANNETTE BROWN** **A WOMAN WITH CLASS** *By Charon Druzen* Date 1-25-94 For English I	**MIGUEL SANCHES** **A traveler** *By Kyli Parstons* Date 6-6-94 For Social Problems Class

If you like, you can dress up the cover of your autobiography with some of these items:

◆ a map showing the places you have lived

◆ a photograph or drawing of someone you admire

◆ favorite drawings or pictures

◆ photographs from your life

◆ an award or important letter you have received

◆ the cover to an album, book, or magazine you enjoy and refer to in your report

Your cover could also be a collage of many things, showing the many ideas covered in your report.

TIP: If you plan to use photographs or other original materials, make copies and use those instead. Your teacher may want to keep your report—it may even be added to your school library collection—so don't use anything that must be returned.

Optional: Giving an Oral Report

Write your outline on note cards. Practice giving your speech in front of a mirror or say it into a tape recorder and listen to it afterward. Your teacher may give everyone a copy of the Speaker Rating Form for Short Report, but you will be rated by only three people: you, your teacher, and another student of your choice. Study the form so you know what you will be rated on and how to use the form when you are asked to rate someone else. If you are not sure what you are supposed to do, ask for help or a demonstration.

Before giving your oral report, you may want to review the lesson on Public Speaking in Part 2 of *Exciting Writing, Successful Speaking.* See if your teacher will let you practice some of the voice and gesture games if you need a refresher course.

Report Writing Quiz

Name _____   Class _____

Period _____   Date _____

Here is a list of the steps used to write a report. See if you can put them in the right order. Write the number of the step beside each one.

___ Make a cover

___ Organize information into an outline

___ Prepare a bibliography

___ Choose a topic

___ Write the final draft (typed or in ink)

___ Revise and edit first draft

___ Turn in the final draft on the due date

___ Collect information

___ Write the first draft

Which two steps were the hardest for you?

_____

_____

Which two steps were the easiest for you?

_____

_____

Are you willing to share your report with future students who need ideas? Would you be willing to leave it at school for storage in a classroom or library file?

☐   Yes, I would leave the original

☐   Yes, I would leave a copy

☐   Yes, if

☐   No

If you would be willing to share your report and leave it at school, be sure to tell your teacher.

Writing a Longer Report

ou're about to begin a project that most students dread: a longer report. But as you'll soon discover, this doesn't have to be a painful, horrible, boring process. For once, you'll get to choose your own topic—a current event or something else that interests you personally. You'll have the chance to use new and different kinds of research materials. The steps are spelled out for you so they are easy to understand, and many are illustrated with examples from a report prepared by a student named Lee. Your teacher will help you when you need help. All you have to do is follow the process shown here and you're practically guaranteed to succeed. When you're through, you'll have a paper you can be proud of, plus you will have learned important skills for the future.

In many ways, your longer report will be similar to the short report (autobiography) you wrote in an earlier lesson. You'll pick up a few new skills—developing research questions, taking notes, preparing a formal bibliography—but if you completed your autobiography, you already know much of what you'll need to write your longer report.

In the process of writing your longer report, you'll collect facts, opinions, and other information from books, magazines, people, computers, brochures, and other sources. As you collect facts to use in your report, you'll actually be conducting research. This may take quite a bit of time, perhaps an entire term. (That is why longer reports are sometimes called term papers.) However, if you spread your work over time and do a little each week, you'll find that it is easy to manage. Along the way, you'll meet interesting people and become an expert on your topic. Your report might even be kept in your school or classroom library and used by future students.

Unlike the autobiography assignment, where the topic (a life) was already decided and the research questions were provided in the Life Questionnaire, you'll be choosing your own topic and creating your own questions. The questions you develop will suggest places to go to collect information.

For example, Lee chose to write his report on the topic of skateboarding. He developed questions like these:

◆ *How can you identify a quality skateboard?*

◆ *How are skateboards made?*

◆ *What are the safety issues connected to skateboarding?*

Once he had written the questions, he knew that he would have to go to the library to answer one, visit a skateboard store to answer another, and meet with the members of a skateboard club or an expert on skateboards to answer another. Can you tell how he figured this out from the questions?

Report writing skills are some of the most important communication skills you'll ever learn. Later in life, you may be asked to write reports by your college instructors or employers. You may need to write reports to apply for grants or prizes. A bank might request a business plan report before giving you a loan to start a project or a business. You will use these writing skills again and again.

Report Writing Review

What are the nine main steps in report writing? Write down as many as you can remember. Check your answers against the list of steps on page 165.

1. _____

2. _____

3. _____

4. _____

5. _____

6. _____

7. _____

8. _____

9. _____

Managing Your Time

When you are assigned a longer report, the due date is usually several weeks away. This may seem like a lot of time. However, due dates *always* come up much more quickly than you expect. If you wait until the last minute to start you're report, you're doomed!

You need to plan and manage your time from the very beginning. It also helps to know how you will be graded on the various parts of your report. Your teacher will give you a Time Management Worksheet showing the five main tasks you'll need to complete and the possible points that will be awarded for each task. Your teacher will tell you how many points are required to earn a grade of A, B, or C.

Choosing Your Topic

When you wrote your autobiography, the topic was easy to write about because it was your story. The Life Questionnaire helped you focus your thoughts and decide what to write. For this assignment, you will choose your own topic and develop your own questions.

Choosing Warm-Up

Imagine that your teacher has collected old magazines from the library and has taken out interesting articles. Your teacher has put the articles into folders labeled "Making a Difference," "Current Problems," "Health," and so on. On the front of each folder, the teacher has written the article titles.

Look at the folders. Which two contain articles on topics you might be interested in writing about? Circle the folder titles. Then underline the article in each folder that you might like to read to collect information for a report.

MAKING A DIFFERENCE

Believing in Yourself

Living the American Dream

Taking Risks for What You Believe

Who Needs Volunteers?

CURRENT PROBLEMS

Hunger and Homelessness

Divorce and New Family

Kids in Custody

Animal Rights

Our Polluted Waterways

Going into Debt Is Painful

HEALTH

Fitness and Body Building

Alcoholism among Teenagers

No Butts about It: New Facts about Cigarettes

Teenagers and Sex

FOODS AND COOKING

Do You Hate Beets?

Pizza—The Ultimate Food

Fast Foods and Your Health

The Five Hottest Hangouts

SPORTS

Diving Championships

Basketball Fever

Baseball Cards Worth $$$

Skateboarding

CULTURAL DIVERSITY AND PREJUDICE

The Ku Klux Klan Today

Life in South Africa

The Return of Anti-Semitism

Prejudice against Native Americans

One Classroom, Seven Languages

MUSIC AND FASHION

Concert Safety

The Top Ten Groups Today

Styles of the Stars

Hair Today, Gone Tomorrow: Teens Shave It Off

Choosing for Real

Now it's time to choose the real topic of your report. You may use one of the article titles you circled. Or brainstorm a list of topic ideas and pick one of those. To be on the safe side, come up with two alternate topics in case your first choice has already been taken.

My first choice topic is: _____

My second choice topic is: _____

My third choice topic is: _____

Why did you pick your first choice topic? Check at least three boxes from the following list. If you can't check three boxes, maybe you need a different first choice topic.

☐   I already know something about the topic.

☐   I know people I can contact for help or information about the topic.

☐   It sounds like fun.

☐   It is something I want to know more about.

Writing Questions and Identifying References

A good report starts with good questions about the topic. Questions guide you in looking for information. They help you focus your research. They suggest books, magazines, or people and places you can contact for information about your topic.

For example, let's say that you are writing a report about people who are homeless. One of your questions might be "How old are most people who live in homeless shelters?" You go to the library to do research and find a list of articles about homelessness in a bibliography. The list looks like this:

"Homeless People: Is a Healthful Diet Possible?"

"The New Homeless: Teenagers"

"Homeless Mothers Train for Jobs"

"Myths about Homelessness"

"The Hidden, Aging Homeless"

Of these articles, which seem most likely to include information that will help you to answer your question?

Now imagine that you're writing a report about laser disks or famous singers. Until you develop your questions, you won't know where to start looking for information.

Questions and References Warm-Up

To experience how questions help focus research efforts, complete this warm-up exercise. Five topics are listed, with sample questions after each topic. For each topic, write two more questions. Then check the question you would find most interesting if you were researching that topic. (This can be one of the sample questions or one of your questions.) Then think about where you would go, what you would read, or the people you might visit to collect information needed to answer the question.

1. Topic: Homelessness

    ☐   What are some of the main problems homeless people face?

    ☐   Should homeless people be allowed to panhandle (ask for money)?

    ☐   Should we as a society do more to help the homeless?

    ☐   _____

    ☐   _____

    Two possible sources of information about the question I checked are:

    _____

    _____

2. Topic: Divorce

    ☐   Why do people get divorced?

    ☐   Is it too easy to get a divorce today?

    ☐   Should we change the laws about divorce or child custody?

    ☐   _____

    ☐   _____

    Two possible sources of information about the question I checked are:

    _____

    _____

3. Topic: Animal Rights

    ☐   Should animals be used in experiments?

    ☐   What are the laws about animal experimentation?

    ☐   What are some companies that experiment on animals? What are some companies that do not experiment on animals?

☐ _____

☐ _____

Two possible sources of information about the question I checked are:

_____

_____

4. Topic: Finding a Job

☐ What should someone do who needs a job in a hurry?

☐ What do "Help Wanted" ads really say?

☐ What is the best way to get ready for a job interview?

☐ _____

☐ _____

Two possible sources of information about the question I checked are:

_____

_____

Questions and References for Real

Start by thinking about your topic. What kinds of questions would you like to ask about it? What kinds of questions would you like to know the answers to? What questions interest you personally? What questions are important to ask? On a separate sheet of paper, brainstorm a list of possible questions. Then pick five and write them here. (Don't fill in the possible references yet.)

1. Question: _____

_____

Possible reference: _____

_____

2. Question: _____

_____

Possible reference: _____

_____

3. Question: _____

_____

Possible reference: _____

_____

4. Question: _____

    _____

    Possible reference: _____

    _____

5. Question: _____

    _____

    Possible reference: _____

    _____

Now circle the number of the question that is most important or interesting to you.

Go back and list five possible references—one for each question. At least two must be books or magazines. You may need to visit a library or store to find these. The rest of your references can be just about any source of expert information. You can use a personal or telephone interview with an expert, a place to visit, a survey, a movie or video, an album cover, a brochure or catalog, or anything else you find.

To help you get started, study Lee's questions and possible references for his skateboarding report. (Notice that one reference lists a shop and another a person.)

1. *Question: How can you identify a quality skateboard?*

    Possible reference: Jason Lowry, student expert on skateboards

2. *Question: How are skateboards made?*

    Possible reference: Skateboard Shop

3. *Question: What are the safety issues connected to skateboarding?*

    Possible reference: Skateboarder News July 5, 1989 issue

Collecting and Organizing Information

As you read and talk to people about your topic, you'll start to collect a lot of information. You will want to keep track of your information so you don't get confused later about who said what or where you found a certain fact or quotation. The best way to keep track of information is by using note cards or special reference pages.

Using Note Cards

Many people prefer to write notes on cards because cards are easy to handle and organize. When you are ready to write your outline, you can put the cards in the order you want. If you decide to reorganize your outline, just rearrange the cards. Also, because note cards are small, you can look at several at the same time by laying them out on a table or desk.

Study the note cards Lee wrote for his report on skateboarding.

CARD A

Source:
Robbins, Suzanne, "20 Tips for Skateboarders," Skateboarder News, July 5, 1989, pages 4-5.

Questions:
What are some facts about skateboard contests?
Are there any safety problems?
What are the costs?

Notes from the article:
People like hanging out with their friends.
Skateboard companies sponsor contests
Freestyle skating is done on flat surfaces and it is like an Olympic contest
People judge you on how smoothly you perform
Skateboarding can be dangerous
One-third of all accidents are cause by lack of experience
Two out of five accidents are caused by people using borrowed boards

---

CARD B

Source:
Jason Lowry, an expert skateboarder at school. I talked to him in person on January 18, 1994

Questions:
What are the costs?

Notes from the interview:
Boards cost about $50 to $200
You can buy kits and assemble them from parts. This can be cheaper
You don't need many tools: only a wrench and a screwdriver
Good brands to buy are Santa Cruz, Powell Puralt, and Rob Rosecap
Helmets cost about $20-35
Elbow pads cost about $10-15
Gloves cost about $10
A quote from Jason: "Helmets are cheaper than hospitals"

CARD C

Source:
Ed Smith, Recreation Counselor, Parks and Recreation Center. I talked to him on the phone on February 2, 1994

Questions:
Are their any skateboarding classes or contests?
Any rules or fees to join?

Notes from the interview:
One contest per year sponsored by rec department—freestyle skating done on flat surfaces
You must wear safety equipment like helmets, elbow pads, and gloves

---

On the next page you'll find 12 miniature note cards with one fact on each card. Suppose you had to organize these facts. You'd have to decide how to group the ideas. Which ideas seem to go together?

To see how note cards can help you organize and group your ideas, photocopy this page and cut out the miniature note cards. Then organize the cards into a possible outline by placing similar ideas in the same group. To help you get started, complete the sample outline on page 195 that already includes the main topics. Or create a different outline and write it on a separate sheet of paper.

MINIATURE REFERENCE CARDS

Photocopy BEFORE cutting!

People like hanging out with their friends	Good brands to buy are Santa Cruz, Powell Puralt, and Rob Rosecap
Skateboarding can be dangerous	Contests sponsored by skateboard manufacturers
Boards cost about $50 to $200	One-third of all accidents are caused by lack of experience
You must wear safety equipment like helmets, elbow pads, and gloves	Two out of five accidents are caused by people using borrowed boards
One contest per year sponsored by rec department	Skateboard companies sponsor contests
Freestyle skating is done on flat surfaces and it is like an Olympic contest	Gloves cost about $10 Elbow pads cost about $10-15 Helmets cost about $20-35

SAMPLE OUTLINE

Theme	Skateboarding

First Main Topic   I.   Build Your Own Boards

Subtopics   A. _____

   B. _____

   C. _____

Second Main Topic   II.   Skateboarding Safety

Subtopics   A. _____

   B. _____

   C. _____

Third Main Topic   III.   Contests

Subtopics   A. _____

   B. _____

   C. _____

Using Special Reference Pages

Some people prefer to use special reference pages rather than note cards because they have more room for writing. Your teacher will give you copies of a reference page you can use.

Tips for using special reference pages:

◆ Put only one source on each page. If you need more room, write on the back or attach another page. (Give that page the same number as your original in case they get separated.)

◆ Try to write something in each blank. If it doesn't apply, write "N/A" (for Not Applicable).

◆ Write down anything that may help you to answer your questions about your report topic.

◆ Write down anything else you find interesting, even if it doesn't relate to your questions. Sometimes this interesting information comes in handy later.

◆ Try to group similar ideas together.

◆ Write down information and ideas in your own words, or copy quotations word-for-word.

Writing Your Outline

Now it is time to organize your ideas and notes into an outline. Follow these steps to create an outline of main headings you will use to organize your notes. You will then use your completed outline to write your report and organize your thoughts for an oral report, if one is required.

STEP 1: Look over your original questions. Turn each question into a statement—a main topic heading.

Here are two examples of how Lee turned questions into headings:

Original question: *Why is skateboarding fun?*

Main topic heading: *Skateboarding Is Fun*

Original question: *Are there many accidents?*

Main topic heading: *Accidents—Beware!*

Tip: Notice that the main topic headings are short, like newspaper headlines.

Now turn your questions into main topic headings:

Original question:

_____

Main topic heading:

_____

Original question:

_____

Main topic heading:

_____

Original question:

_____

Main topic heading:

_____

Original question:

_____

Main topic heading:

_____

Original question:

_____

Main topic heading:

_____

Transfer your main topic headings to the Report Outline form your teacher will give you. Don't worry about the Introduction and Conclusion; you'll do those later.

STEP 2:   Organize your note cards or special reference pages into groups that match your main topic headings. Read through your notes. You will use some of these facts or details as subtopics in your outline.

As you try to decide which facts or details to use as subtopics, ask yourself these questions:

◆   What would be most interesting to the reader?

◆   What do I think is most important?

Write your subtopics under the main topic headings on the Report Outline.

Here is what Lee's outline for his skateboarding report looked like at this stage:

SKATEBOARDING OUTLINE

I.   *Introduction (DO LAST)*

II.   *Skateboarding is fun*

    A.   *You hang out with friends.*

    B.   *Free-style can be done anywhere. It is wild. There are jumps.*

    C.   *It is exciting like the Olympic sports.*

    D.   *You can get lessons from friends or at stores.*

III. *Accidents—Beware!*

    A.   *Caused by not having experience.*

    B.   *One-third of accidents caused by people using borrowed boards.*

    C.   *Should wear helmet, elbow guards, and gloves.*

IV.   *How much does it cost?*

    A.   *Boards cost about $50 to $200.*

    B.   *You can buy kits and assemble them from parts. This can be cheaper.*

    C.   *You don't need many tools: only a wrench and a screwdriver.*

    D.   *Helmets cost about $20-35, elbow pads cost about $10-15, gloves cost about $10.*

V.   *Conclusion (DO LAST)*

STEP 3:   Decide what to do with any leftover notes, facts, or details. First, see if any of the unused notes and facts can be grouped together. If they can, what main topic heading could you write to describe this new group? Go ahead and add a new heading to your outline. If this doesn't work, look over your outline and see if any leftover notes can be put under existing main topic headings. If this doesn't work...you can't always use every fact you collect.

Writing Your Introduction and Conclusion

It's easier to write your introduction and conclusion *after* you know your main topics and subtopics. Use these tips and warm-ups to get started. Try to fill in all of the blanks.

The Introduction

1. Introduce your topic.

    This report is about _____.

2. Tell why your topic is important. Avoid using the words "I," "we," or "you."

    _____ *(your topic) is one of the most important* _____
    facing _____ *today.*

3. Include an interesting fact or question which will grab your reader's attention right away.

    Most people aren't aware that every year _____ *people would
    like to* _____.

    Or:

    Have you ever wondered why _____?

4. Tell what is in your report. List the three most important topics.

    This report covers the three main ideas, _____, _____,
    and _____.

5. Tell the most important question answered in your report. This is sometimes called your hypothesis. It is the question you were able to collect the most information about.

    *This report attempts to answer the question, "*_____
    _____?"*

Here is Lee's outlined introduction. Notice that he simply repeats the main topics in his outline.

I. *Introduction*

    A. *Skateboarding can be a lot of fun.*

    B. *There are contests.*

    C. *Safety is also important.*

    D. *It costs some money.*

The Conclusion

1. Use a word or phrase that describes your topic, then repeat one of your most important ideas.

    In summary, this report shows that the most important thing about _____ *is* _____ .

2. Ask the reader a question or state an opinion. When stating an opinion, avoid using the words "I," "me," or "you."

    Have you ever wondered about _____?

    This report suggests that the one of the most important problems faced by _____ *is* _____ .

3. If you included a question in your introduction, give the answer.

    The answer to " _____ *"*
    appears to be _____ .

Here is Lee's outlined conclusion. Notice that he states three opinions.

V. *Conclusion*

    A. *A good all-around sport.*

    B. *Lots of fun.*

    C. *Can learn many useful things.*

When you have finished outlining your introduction and conclusion, transfer them to your Report Outline.

Writing Your Report

There are only a few steps left to completing your report. You'll write and revise a first (rough) draft. Then you'll type your final draft or write it in ink. Finally, you'll add a cover and a bibliography.

Writing the First Draft

Follow these guidelines:

1.   Write in pencil (or type on a computer).

2.   Write on every other line so there is room for changes and corrections.

3.   Write at least the same number of paragraphs as there are topic headings in your outline (including the introduction and conclusion). In other words, if your outline includes five main topics, your report must include at least seven paragraphs. You may write more paragraphs than the number of your topic headings, but you cannot write fewer paragraphs than that number.

     As you write, you'll be adding words to the information listed in your outline. This is called expanding your outline. You'll find an example of how to do this on page 179 in Writing a Short Report: The (Auto)Biography.

     If you use direct quotations from references, be sure to include quotation marks. Indent longer quotations. Longer indented quotations do not need quotation marks.

     Here is an example from Lee's report:

     According to the brochure, "Skateboarding Basics":

     Skateboarding is a national pastime that is growing by leaps and bounds. As it skyrockets in interest, health costs have also risen. As a result, insurance companies now ask families to list members who skateboard.

4.   When you have completed your first draft, go back over it and make any changes or corrections. Then read the draft out loud. Does it sound right? Does each paragraph have an opening sentence and a closing sentence?

5.   Prepare your bibliography according to the guidelines on pages 201–204.

Finishing Your Report

1. When your first draft has been edited and corrected, write your final draft. Use ink, a typewriter, or a word processor.

2. Make a cover. Review the ideas and suggestions on page 181 in Writing a Short Report: The (Auto)Biography. Here are three more examples of simple covers. Remember that each cover must include your title, your name, the date written (or due date), and your class.

SKATEBOARDING

A thrill to be safely enjoyed

By Karen Remson

Submitted 6-6-94
For Science Class

One Classroom, Seven Languages

How a school welcomes immigrants

BY HECTOR VALEZ

Date 1/25/94
For Comp I

THE HOMELESS

A PROBLEM WE ALL NEED TO FACE

By Tommi Budde

Date 4-4-94
For Volunteer Service Class

Save Your Outline!

Even when you think you are finished with your outline, save it. Often teachers ask students to give an oral report on their research. In this way, students can share their report findings with the rest of the class.

Your outline all by itself is an "instant speech." Transfer it onto small note cards. Practice giving your speech in front of a mirror or into a tape recorder. The Speaker Rating Form for Short Report that your teacher may give you may also be used to evaluate longer reports.

Preparing a Formal Bibliography

If you take notes on special reference pages, you will probably gather all of the information you need to prepare a professional bibliography. If you are not using special reference pages, you should be recording bibliographical information on your note cards or in a notebook. Your report will not be complete without a bibliography.

There are several ways to format bibliographical references. It doesn't really matter which one you use, as long as you include all of the necessary information—and as long as you are consistent. For example, all book references should follow the same format. Your teacher may give you a format to use. If this is the case, follow that format exactly or you may lose points off of your final report score. If your teacher does not specify a format, here are examples for the different types of references. List your references in alphabetical order in your final bibliography.

Book References

Include this information:

- Author's name (last name first)
- Title of book (underlined)
- Name of publisher
- City of publication
- Year of publication (or copyright year)
- The pages you used in your research

Example:

Jerome, Lloyd. <u>The Complete Skateboard Cookbook.</u> Skateboard Press Inc. Pensacola, FL: 1992. Pages 45-67.

Book Chapter References

Include this information:

- Author's name (last name first)
- Chapter title (in quotation marks)
- Title of book (underlined, with "In")
- Name of publisher
- City of publication
- Year of publication (or copyright year)
- The chapter pages

Example:

Yellowstone, Thomas. "Skateboarding Safety." In <u>Sports: Hazardous To Your Health?</u> Series Press Inc. New York, NY: 1994. Pages 22-43.

Magazine Article References

Include this information:

- Author's name (last name first)
- Title of article (in quotation marks)
- Title of magazine (underlined)
- Date and year of publication
- The pages you used in your research

Example:

Robbins, Suzanne, "20 Tips for Skateboarders," <u>Skateboarder News,</u> July 5, 1989, pages 4-5.

Newspaper Article References

Include this information:

◆ Author's name (last name first)

◆ Title of article (in quotation marks)

◆ Name of newspaper (underlined)

◆ Date and year of publication

◆ The pages you used in your research

Example:

Wise, Randy. "Area Skateboarders Compete in Nationals." The Tumwater Times. October 13, 1993. Page 8D.

Brochure References

Include this information:

◆ Title of brochure (in quotation marks)

◆ Company or agency that prepared the brochure

◆ Date (if available)

Example:

"Rating Skateboarding Helmets." A brochure prepared by Headhuggers Helmet Co. 1992.

Film or Video References

Include this information:

◆ Title of film or video

◆ Other information that would help the reader

"Skateboarding Championships 1991." A 60-minute video produced by the Skateboarding Association.

Personal Interview References

Include this information:

◆ The name of the person you interviewed (last name first)

◆ Where the interview took place

◆ The date of the interview

◆ Other information that would help the reader

Examples:

Lowry, Jason. Personal interview at North Thurston High School. January 18, 1994.

McCullough, Adrienne. Telephone interview. January 5, 1994.

Student Paper References

Include this information:

- Author's name (last name first)
- Title of paper (in quotation marks)
- School library or class
- Date on paper

Example:

Howard, Tony. "Sports on Skates." Kennedy High School Library. Dated May 20, 1993.

Sound Recording References

Include this information:

- The name of the performer(s)
- If music audio: the title of the recording (underlined)
- If spoken word audio: the title of the recording (in quotation marks)
- The company
- The date of release (if available)
- The length (if available)

Examples:

Summer, Bobby. Skateboarding Songs. Sport Records SK142. 1976.

Emmett, Tiffany. "How I Won the Skateboarding Championship." Washton, MA. Winners Corp. 1992. 30-minute cassette.

Computer Program References

Include this information:

- Title of program (in quotation marks)
- Version number
- Name of company
- City where company is located

Example:

"Skateboarding Down Elm Street." Version 5.3. Almost Real Games Co. Pleasant, VT.

Index

A

Acceptance speeches, 90-91
Acting. *See* Drama; Script writing;
 Theater games
Advertising writing, 6, 29-44
 details in, 31
 good copy, 34-37
 newspaper, 38-39
 for personal ad, 32-33
 for product, 32
 public service announcement, 40-43
 radio, 40-43
 television, 44
 See also Script writing
Artwork
 in journals, 22
 See Cartoons; Floor plan drawings
Autobiographies and biographies, 144,
 163-183
 bibliography, 180
 brainstorming, 165
 conclusion, 177-179
 cover making, 181
 drafts, 179-180
 finishing, 179-182
 introduction, 177-179
 oral report, 182
 outlining, 172-177
 questionnaire, 165-172
 quiz, 183
 references, 165
 writing steps, 164-165

B

Bibliographies, for reports, 180,
 201-204
Biographies. *See* Autobiographies and
 biographies
Book reports, 144, 160-162
 oral reports, 162
 outlining, 161-162
 See also Reading journals
Brainstorming
 and essay writing, 72-74
 as prewriting tool, 12, 76
 and speech writing, 92-93, 95-96
Breathing games, as public speaking
 warm-up, 81-82

C

Capitalization, 15
Cartoons, 136
Character analysis, 70, 117, 122-132
Charades, as public speaking warm-up,
 69, 86-87
Closing sentences, 78
Communication skills, 1
 See also Public speaking

D

Dialogue, writing, 105-110
Drafts
 for poems, 56-57
 for reporting, 200
 for writing, 13-16
 See also Final drafts; First drafts
Drama
 appreciation, 70, 116-118

See also Script writing; Theater games

Drawings. *See* Artwork

E

Editing
  final drafts, 15-16, 79
  first drafts, 14-15, 78
  stories, 139
Essay writing, 71-72, 75-79

F

Final drafts, editing and revising, 15-16, 79
First drafts
  editing and revising, 14-15, 78
  writing, 77-78
Floor plan drawings, as writing exercise, 71, 73, 75
Four step writing process. *See under* Writing

G

Gestures, and public speaking, 80, 86-87

H

Home assignment, for essay writing, 69, 71-79

I

Interviews, 46
Introductions, 88-90

J

Journal writing, 5, 17-28
  details in, 18-19
  endings, 23-24
  example, 21
  pictures in, 22
  reading coach, 19
  rules, 20
  topics, 24-28
  word count chart, 20

K

Kimeldorf, Martin, 208

L

Letter writing, 10
List writing, 5, 7-10
  example, 8
  and letter writing, 10

M

Music, and writing, 72

N

Newsletter projects, 70, 119-121
  example, 120
Newspaper ads, 38-39
Note cards, for term papers, 192-194

O

Opening sentences, 77-78
Organization, as prewriting tool, 12-13, 76
Outlines
  for autobiographies/biographies, 172-177
  for book reports, 161-162
  for reports, 195, 196-198, 201
  for scripts, 114-115
  for speeches, 91-98

P

Pantomimes. *See* Theater games
Pet peeve speeches, 98
Pictures. *See* Artwork
Plays. *See* Drama; Script writing; Theater games
Plot analysis, 70, 133-139
Plotting, and script writing, 110-113
PoemBuilder, 58-66
Poetry, 6, 45-66
  characteristics of, 47-52
  drafts, 56-57, 62
  examples, 65
  exercises, 52-56
  reasons to write, 46-47
  revising, 64
  13-line, 56-57
  title for, 66
  topics, 58-60
Power writing, 5, 9
Prewriting, 12-13, 76-77
Public service announcement writing, 40-43
Public speaking, 69, 80-99
  beginning speeches, 88-91
  and communication skills, 80
  getting started, 80-91
  warm-ups, 69, 81-83, 86-87
  vs. writing, 80
  See also Speech writing
Punctuation, 16

Q

Quizzes, on report writing, 183

R

Radio advertising writing, 40-43
Reading aloud, first drafts, 78
Reading journals, 160-61.
    See also Book reports
Reporting, 143-204
    longer reports, 143, 144, 184-204
    See also Book reports; Surveys;
        Term papers
Research papers. *See* Term papers
Revising, first drafts, 78
Rough drafts. *See* First drafts

S

Sales speeches, 99
Script writing, 70, 105-118
    outlining, 114-115
    rules, 116
    symbols in, 118
    See also Advertising writing;
        Drama; Theater games
Setting, in stories, 133
Skits. *See* Drama; Script writing;
    Theater games
Speech making. *See* Public speaking
Speech writing, 69, 91-99
    outlining, 91-98
    topics, 98-99
    See also Public speaking
Spelling, 16
Story assignments, 70, 122-139
Surveys, 143, 145-159
    designing, 147-53
    example, 154-56
    PoemBuilder, 58-60
    questions, 146-47
    report writing, 157-59
    types of questions, 146-147

T

Television advertising writing, 44
Term papers, 184-204
    bibliography, 201-204
    conclusion, 198-199
    drafts, 200-201
    finishing, 201-204
    information collection, 191-195
    introduction, 198-199

outlining, 196-198, 201
questions writing, 188-191
references, 188-191, 195, 202-204
review, 185
time management, 186
topic choice, 186-188
writing steps, 164-165
Theater games, 70, 100-104
    See also Drama; Script writing
Time management, for term papers,
    186
Tone-of-voice, and public speaking,
    84-85
Tongue-twisters, as public speaking
    warm-up, 69, 83

V

Visualizing, and essay writing, 71, 72

W

Warm-ups
    for advertising, 32-34
    for autobiographies/biographies,
        174-176
    for four-step writing, 11-12
    for plot analysis, 133
    for public speaking, 69, 81-83, 86-87
    for report writing, 186-187, 189-190
    for survey questions, 146-147
    See also Theater games
Word counting, and journal writing, 20
Word play, as poetry, 50-52
Writing
    four step process, 5, 11-16, 75-79
    vs. speaking, 80
    types of, 5
    See also Drafts; Editing; Prewriting;
        Revising; specific types of writing,
        e.g. Journal writing

About the Author

artin Kimeldorf is the author of over 15 books and reports on the topics of job finding, leisure finding, community service, journal writing, and recreational drama. He holds Bachelor of Science degrees in technology education and liberal arts from Oregon State University and a Master's Degree in special education from Portland State University. He received the Literati Award from the *International Journal of Career Management* for Best Paper of the Year and has won other awards for teaching and playwriting. His hobbies include wood carving, painting, and magic. Martin lives with his wife, Judy, and their dog, Mitzi, in Tumwater, Washington.

More Free Spirit Books

The Kid's Guide to Social Action:
How to Solve the Social Problems You Choose—and Turn Creative Thinking into Positive Action
by Barbara A. Lewis
A comprehensive guide to making a difference in the world. Teaches letter-writing, interviewing, speechmaking, fundraising, lobbying, getting media coverage and more. Ages 10 and up.

208 pp; illus.; B&W photos; s/c; 8 1/2"x11"; ISBN 0-915793-29-6; $14.95

A Gebra Named Al
by Wendy Isdell
A witty, intelligent story that blends fantasy and adventure with basic principles of mathematics and chemistry. Ages 11 and up.

136 pp; s/c; 5 1/2"x7 1/2" ISBN 0-915793-58-X; $4.95

School Power:
Strategies for Succeeding in School
by Jeanne Shay Schumm, Ph.D. and Marguerite Radencich, Ph.D.
Covers getting organized, taking notes, studying smarter, writing better, following directions, handling home-work, managing long-term assignments, and more. Ages 11 and up.

132 pp; illus.; B&W photos; s/c; 8 1/2"x11"; ISBN 0-915793-42-3; $11.95

Girls and Young Women Leading the Way:
20 True Stories About Leadership
by Frances A. Karnes, Ph.D., and Suzanne M. Bean, Ph.D.
These inspiring stories from girls and young women ages 8 to 21 prove that leadership is for everyone, that leadership opportunities are every-where, and that leadership has many faces and takes many forms. Ages 11 and up.

168 pp; B&W photos; s/c; 6"x9" ISBN 0-915793-52-0; $11.95

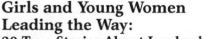

Making the Most of Today:
Daily Readings for Young People on Self-Awareness, Creativity, and Self-Esteem
by Pamela Espeland and Rosemary Wallner
Guides young people through a year of positive thinking, problem-solving, and practical lifeskills. Ages 11 and up.

392 pp; s/c; 4"x7" ISBN 0-915793-33-4; $8.95

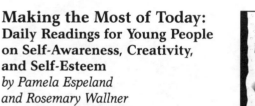

Fighting Invisible Tigers:
A Stress Management Guide for Teens
by Earl Hipp
Advice for young people who feel frustrated, overwhelmed, or depressed about life and want to do something about it. Ages 11 and up.

120 pp; illus.; s/c; 6"x9" ISBN 0-915793-04-0; $9.95

To place an order, or to request a free SELF-HELP FOR KIDS® catalog, write or call:

Free Spirit Publishing Inc.
400 First Avenue North, Suite 616
Minneapolis, MN 55401-1730
612-338-2068
800-735-7323